Ox in the Ditch

Bible Interpretation
as the Foundation of Christian Ethics

Kerry Duke

Publishing Designs, Inc.
Huntsville, Alabama

Publishing Designs, Inc.
P. O. Box 3241
Huntsville, Alabama 35810

Printed in the United States of America

Library of Congress Cataloging-in-Publication Data

Duke, Kerry, 1959-
    Ox in the ditch : Bible interpretation as the foundation of
Christian ethics / Kerry Duke.
        p. cm.
    Includes bibliographical references.
    ISBN 0-929540-16-6 : $6.95
    1. Christian ethics—Biblical teaching. 2. Ethics in the Bible.
3. Bible—Criticism, interpretation, etc. I. Title.
BS680.E84D85   1993
241'.2—dc20   93-24149
                                                        CIP

To my wife LeAnn,
my rock, my joy,
the woman who has filled
my life with
happiness and confidence.

Contents

Foreword vii

Preface ix

PART ONE: IDENTIFYING THE PRINCIPLE

1 The Nature of Biblical Revelation 3
  Biblical Infallibility
  The Diversity of the Scriptures
  Distribution of Subject Matter
  The Conciseness of Scripture

2 Explanation of the Principle 17
  Analogies
  Synthesizing Biblical Material
  Types of Qualifications
  Areas Which Must Deal With the Principle

3 Evaluation of Common Approaches 37
  The Rejection of Seeking Solutions
  Common Sense
  Counting Verses
  Love as the Norm: Situation Ethics
  The Question of Moral Dilemmas
  Guidance of the Holy Spirit
  Proof-Texting
  The Danger of Personal Bias

PART TWO: BIBLICAL PRECEDENTS

4 Qualification and the Covenants 63
    Convenant Amenability
    Circumstantial Qualification
    Moral Principles

5 Qualification in Realms of Delegated Authority ... 77
    The Principle of Delegated Authority in Scripture
    Delegated Authority–Qualified Authority

6 Qualification by Priority of Principle 87
    Jesus and the Sabbath Labor Law
    Corban and the Fifth Commandment

PART THREE: APPLICATION

7 Test Cases: Ethical Problems Examined in
    Light of the Principle 111
    Is Lying Ever Justified?
    Unscriptural Marriages and the Demands of
        Love
    The Abortion Controversy
    Obligations to Family Members

8 Are there Qualifications of the Principle of
    Qualification? 135
    Qualification: A Means for Justifying any Belief?
    Does the Principle Have Practical Value in
        Choosing the Better of Two Actions?
    Do Ethical Dilemmas Actually Occur on the
        Practical Level?
Bibliography 143

Foreword

I have known Kerry Duke for many years even though he is still considered a young man. I have known him in different positions. First, I knew him as Kerry Duke, a friend. Second, I knew him as Kerry Duke, one of our students at Tennessee Bible College. Third, I knew him as Kerry Duke, one of my students. Fourth, I knew him as Kerry Duke, our library overseer. Fifth, I knew him as Kerry Duke, one of our part-time teachers. Sixth, I knew him as Kerry Duke, one of our full-time teachers. Now I know him as Kerry Duke, Dean of the undergraduate school at Tennessee Bible College and professor of Bible, logic, and philosophy.

Kerry Duke is one of the most diligent students I have ever known. He studies for hours each day. God has blessed him with one of the keenest minds to be found. He is truly a scholar.

In Kerry we find a mixture of goodness. He is humble, teachable, sincere, unassuming, balanced, and forever seeking the truth in all things. He stands like a rock for what he believes to be right but is the very first one to apologize when he is convinced he is wrong. He is one of the best team men I have ever known when it comes to our work at Tennessee Bible College. He loves students and takes a personal interest in each of them.

Any time Kerry Duke speaks I am ready to listen, for I know he will have something to say that will enlighten. I feel the same way about his writings. He leaves no stones unturned and even though he is scholarly yet his writings are simple and one is able to grasp them.

His new book, *Ox in the Ditch*, will help every truth seeker to understand the Bible better. Kerry Duke believes that the Bible is plenarily and verbally inspired. You can know a friend of God's Word is at work when you read his material. I cannot commend this work too highly.

Dr. Duke received all of his degrees from Tennessee Bible College. He holds the B.A. degree in Bible and the M.A. and Ph.D. degrees in Christian Doctrine and Apologetics. He has a lovely wife, LeAnn, and four very fine children.

Malcolm L. Hill, President
Tennessee Bible College
Cookeville, Tennessee

Preface

Bible interpretation is a study of relationships—the relationships between its various parts. Before we can understand a verse of Scripture, we must see how its words relate to each other. We arrive at its meaning by observing how the nouns, verbs, and other parts of speech fit together. But grammar is only one phase in interpretation. The verse must be studied in light of the verses that surround it. We must study the Bible by paragraph, since a paragraph usually contains several related sentences which express a central thought. Care must be given to note the connections between these sentences.

Though the work of interpretation may appear to be finished at this point, it actually has just begun. The passage under consideration must also be studied in relation to the section of the book in which it occurs, the purpose of the book, and the testament of which it is a part. Beyond these steps is an equally vital task: interpreting the passage in light of the entirety of God's Word.

Hermeneutics emphasizes this interrelatedness of individual parts of the Bible, maintaining that any thought unit is to be interpreted in light of the overall message of God's Word. A part of Scripture cannot genuinely be studied in isolation from the whole. In true Bible interpretation, no verse is an island.

The idea for this book came from a study of Jesus' discussion of the Sabbath labor law in Matthew 12. In showing how this law applied to the Jews, Jesus appealed to Old Testament principles which shed light on the meaning of the law. He taught the necessity of fitting together relevant information on the subject. Since one of the circumstances He mentioned was livestock in the ditch on the Sabbath day, this example is an appropriate title for this book.

The task of fitting together statements occurring in distant contexts is a persistent challenge in Bible interpretation. An interpreter often finds that the meaning of a biblical statement is drastically affected by verses in other books. The effect observed when one Bible verse limits the application of another is called qualification. This means that an apparently broad statement of Scripture may be quite restricted in application. It also means that the course of action required by a verse may not be appropriate for every situation. As a type of relationship between verses that is encountered in the broader area of synthesizing biblical information, the subject of qualification is a critical area of concern in hermeneutics.

How are qualifications in Scripture to be detected? What criteria are given in Scripture that enable us to distinguish the qualifying verse from the qualified verse? In addressing these questions, this study will follow a three-step plan. First, an explanation of the problem will be given showing the necessity of this topic in hermeneutics, the nature of qualification in Scripture, and the errors of proposed ways of dealing with the problem. Second, a survey of major areas of biblical examples of qualification is presented to arrive at guidelines for ascertaining the relationship when it is not explicitly stated. Third, the information derived in part two will be applied to significant current issues in which the principle of qualification has been incorrectly applied. Attention also will be given in this section to special considerations regarding the application of the principle.

This book is designed to introduce the principle of qualification and to examine some more difficult matters associated with it. Though its application in ethics plays a substantial role in this study, the fundamental issue under consideration is hermeneutical. In discussing the details of this subject I have attempted to employ terminology that is as simple yet accurate as possible. Scripture quotations are from the New King James Version (1982, Nelson).

Of the numerous persons who have helped me in writing this book, several deserve special recognition. I am indebted to Glenn Ramsey for the countless hours he spent typing the text and for the important advice he provided. James McGill regularly gave direction regarding its readability in his typically encouraging manner. Malcolm Hill, who wrote the foreword, spent extra time challenging my reasoning in regard to the issues discussed in chapter seven. I owe much to him because of the fatherly interest he has taken in my life and in my work. Ben Gore and Thomas Eaves offered valuable advice concerning specific points of Greek and hermeneutics. Students at Tennessee Bible College were an important sounding board, and I was greatly encouraged by their interest and observations. I would also like to express appreciation to Tim and Connie McHenry, Bobby Delk and Nita Flatt for reading the manuscript. I am also indebted to James Andrews of Publishing Designs for suggesting the title. From my perspective, these contributions were invaluable. From the reader's viewpoint, any weaknesses in the following pages should be attributed solely to me. This volume is extended in prayerful hope that the reader will arrive at a more complete understanding of the will of God.

PART
ONE

IDENTIFYING
THE PRINCIPLE

1

The Nature of
Biblical Revelation

The importance of engaging in a study of the principle of qualification lies in the unique character of the Scriptures. The Bible is an ancient document that serves as a permanent revelation of God's will for man. Since the faith has been "once for all delivered to the saints" (Jude 3), the contents of the Bible remain the same. As interpreters, we are left only with the information contained in the Bible as it is. No supplemental revelation will be given to clarify the existing one. Consequently, we should handle it reverently and honestly as the sole and final source of religious authority.

The antiquity and literary style of the Bible have given rise to doubts concerning its adequacy as a guide for modern man. After all, the secularly oriented interpreter reasons, the historical-cultural setting of Bible writings is vastly different from ours, and the problems of the original recipients of Bible books are not the burning issues of today. Many of its modes of expression are foreign to Western civilization. As a result, intensive efforts to interpret Scripture with specific current application have been largely abandoned. This chapter upholds the Bible as the perfectly consistent and comprehensive guide for the Christian life. Also, it emphasizes the need for thoroughness in interpretation because of the manner in which the Bible was written.

Biblical Infallibility

Every interpreter approaches the Bible with certain presuppositions.[1] These presuppositions affect the method of interpretation, the conclusions drawn, and the significance attached to those conclusions by the interpreter. A central presupposition is the interpreter's view of the inspiration of Scripture. If Bible teaching is not infallible in its entirety, then the process of synthesizing biblical information is needless and its results questionable. But if in fact the Bible is infallible, the most careful and thorough effort should characterize this step in interpretation. Since this study proceeds from the latter of these positions, a few observations concerning infallibility are appropriate.

Behind the doctrine of biblical infallibility is the plenary aspect of the inspiration of Scripture, the view that all parts of the Bible are equally inspired. This property is affirmed both directly and indirectly by biblical authors. Paul explicitly stated, "All Scripture is given by inspiration of God" (II Tim. 3:16). That Bible writers shared this view is evident from how they refer to each other's writings. In warning his readers concerning those who perverted Paul's hard sayings, Peter classified the Pauline epistles with "the rest of the Scriptures" (II Pet. 3:16). Paul recognized the statement of Jesus recorded in Luke 10:7, "The laborer is worthy of his wages," as Scripture (I Tim. 5:18). The numerous quotations of the Old Testament found in the New Testament indicate the status given to those books by inspired first century writers. Even the seemingly insignificant saying, "You are gods" (Ps. 82:6), was declared by Jesus to be "Scripture" that "cannot be broken" (John 10:34-35).

The denial of plenary inspiration has serious implications about Christians and the God they serve. If some parts of

---

[1]The word *presupposition* does not necessarily mean "unproven assumption." For instance, to say that an interpreter presupposes the inspiration of Scripture is not to imply that he proceeds on the basis of blind faith. Prophecy, unity, scientific foreknowledge and other unique attributes of the Bible demonstrate its divine origin.

Scripture are fallible, Christians are burdened with the hopeless task of separating the inspired from the uninspired parts. Upon what basis is this distinction to be made? Such a revelation would be unreliable as a guide for Christians. More importantly, a denial of plenary inspiration is an indictment of God. One cannot criticize a book without casting reflection on its author. To suggest that God delivered a partially inspired Bible is to say that He is unfair and less than all-powerful. A fallible Bible means that God has placed man in the predicament of being dependent upon the Bible for salvation but incapable of being certain as to what the Word of God really is. In addition to these implications, opposers of plenary inspiration cannot escape the charge of inconsistency when they quote Scripture to prove a point. What if the passage cited is one of the "fallible" parts of Scripture?

On the other hand, the acceptance of the doctrine of infallibility has enormous implications for the interpreter. Three inherent properties of an infallible revelation are of special concern in interpretation. One such property is *internal consistency*. Though inner coherence alone does not verify a system of thought, consistency is an essential aspect of truth. In spite of how little we know about a book, we know that it is fallible if it is self-contradictory. If the Bible is the inerrant word of God, it cannot contain genuine contradictions. Any Bible student encounters difficulties in attempting to harmonize the Scriptures, but unresolved problems in interpretation reflect our own ignorance and not some weakness in God's manner of communication. Often the key to solving the apparent discrepancy is earnest study of the context of the passages in question. Later knowledge also clears up many difficult items of interpretation, though we must admit that we will die with numerous unanswered questions about the Bible. For humility's sake it is worthwhile to remember that we do not really "harmonize" the Scriptures. Regardless of alleged discrepancies, the Bible is harmonious and we merely recognize this harmony when we arrive at a "solution" to a difficult matter of interpretation.

The fact of harmony in Scripture exists independently of our ability or inability to grasp it. An understanding of this fact enables us to rely confidently on the Scriptures as a perfectly consistent guide.

Another characteristic of a perfect guide is *comprehensiveness*. A fundamental premise of this book is that the Bible contains every needed principle for Christian living. This property of all-sufficiency is affirmed by New Testament writers:

> All Scripture is given by inspiration of God, and is profitable for doctrine, for reproof, for correction, for instruction in righteousness, that the man of God may be complete, thoroughly equipped for every good work (II Tim. 3:16-17).

> . . . His divine power has given to us all things that pertain to life and godliness, through the knowledge of Him who called us by glory and virtue (II Pet. 1:3).

A comprehensive revelation is the only type of guide that corresponds to the needs of Christians concerning doctrine and life. How can worship that is acceptable to God be determined without a complete guide? How can everyday ethical decisions be properly made unless we have the principles necessary for making those decisions? Without a comprehensive guide, we are adrift on life's sea with a faulty compass.

Failure to appreciate this property of Scripture, together with the popular demand for a relevant and practical message, has contributed to a distressing tendency among Bible-believing people. The Bible is no longer looked upon as an adequate source of principles for Christian growth. Instead, a growing reliance has developed upon specialists in every area of life—all for spiritual development. While specialists in specific problem areas may provide legitimate help for special needs, an important fact should be remembered: any true principle of spiritual development they offer has its origin in Scripture, not in men. Humans merely discover these truths. Specialists in psychology and sociology should be considered *assistants* for finding scriptural solutions to spiritual problems, as commentaries should be used as aids to understanding Scripture and not as ends in themselves. To do otherwise is to make the disastrous mistake of exalting human wisdom over the perfect wisdom of God.

Of special concern to interpreters is the property of *understandability* in divine revelation. Unless the Scriptures are understandable, Bible study is useless. But the word *revelation* itself refers to a message that has been made known, and this characteristic of Scripture is often affirmed by Bible writers: Jesus said, "Whoever reads, let him understand" (Matt. 24:15). Paul said, "I wrote before in a few words, by which, when you read, you may understand my knowledge in the mystery of Christ" (Eph. 3:3-4).

A major reason for the abandonment of serious Bible study today is the denial that the Scriptures can be understood. Objections against this property of Scripture take several forms. One of the most common of these criticisms is that if the Bible can be understood by all, then why does such a wide range of religious division exist? A thorough discussion of the reasons for the fragmented doctrinal state of those professing to follow Christ is beyond the scope of this study. This condition does not negate the property of understandability in Scripture because religious division is human in origin. The divided state of religion cannot be blamed on God because He is not "the author of confusion" (I Cor. 14:33). God created man with the ability to reason correctly with the Scriptures and come to the knowledge of the truth. The requirement for attaining this knowledge is not the level of genius, but a sincere desire to obey God:

> If anyone wants to do His will, he shall know concerning the doctrine, whether it is from God or whether I speak on my own authority (John 7:17).

Another objection to this characteristic of the Scriptures is the claim that human language is an imperfect vehicle for conveying divine thought. It is considered inadequate for accurately transmitting the will of God. But this objection turns on the critic, since he uses this same medium to communicate! If all human language is as ambiguous as the objector assumes, how can the objection itself be accurately interpreted? The important scriptural fact concerning this charge is that God created man with the ability to communicate. Otherwise, the basis for human relationships is undermined. "Who has made man's mouth? . . . Have not I, the Lord" (Exod. 4:11)?

Did Peter suggest that Scripture cannot be understood without outside assistance? His statement, "No prophecy of Scripture is of any private interpretation" (II Pet. 1:20), may be misconstrued to this end. The explanatory verse that follows, however, indicates that Peter was stressing the origin of Scripture, not its interpretation: "For prophecy never came by the will of man, but holy men of God spoke as they were moved by the Holy Spirit" (v. 21).

In addition, this view of the verse is self-defeating, since it urges us to *understand* what is alleged to be the meaning of the verse!

The Diversity of the Scriptures

The fact that the Bible is a "Book of books" demands constant attention in interpretation. Each of its sixty-six books is unique, contributing a necessary element in the development of the theme of Scripture. When synthesizing information from various locations in the Bible, the interpreter must be alert to differences in these books. Differences in the date of the setting of the books and in the literary type of the books are particularly significant in regard to interpretation.

The modern reader of the Bible is sometimes unaware that the Scriptures did not always consist of the completed form we now possess. The biblical writings were composed gradually during a sixteen-century period. God spoke "at various times and in different ways" (Heb. 1:2). Had He desired to do so, God could have delivered a revelation containing every needed principle of righteousness at the very beginning of man's existence. In this scenario, Adam would have possessed a Bible—a Bible far different, however, from the one in use today.

God has delivered a revelation in which principles of righteousness and specific legislation are weaved into the historical development of the redemptive plan. The characters, places, and events provided the circumstantial means by which divine truth was conveyed. Without its recorded history, the Bible loses the motivational effectiveness and instructional simplicity so characteristic of the story. The value of history is often affirmed in the New Testament. Paul wrote, "For whatever things were written before were written for our learning . . ." (Rom. 15:4). He further said, "Now all these things happened to them as examples, and they were written for our admonition . . ." (I Cor. 10:11).

The preparatory aspect of the Old Testament also made a lengthy time span for its composition necessary. As God prepared mankind for the coming of the Messiah, He dealt with man according to his current situation. The contents of the revelation correspond to the state of man. Accordingly, the period from Adam to Moses (Patriarchy) prepared the Hebrews for the Mosaic law, and the Mosaic law prepared the Jews for the gospel of Christ. The law of Moses was in Paul's description a *paidagogos* (Gal. 3:24-25), a guardian or custodian of the Jewish nation to which the Jews were subject until the coming of faith. An important aspect of this preparation involves the promises, types, and prophecies in the Old Testament regarding the Messianic kingdom. The time between the making and fulfilling of these future indicators was often centuries.

The result of the gradual composition of the Bible during this period is that the interpreter encounters numerous changes as he studies different Bible books. The background of Bible books often differs in culture, language, geography, and political circumstances. More importantly, moral and religious legislation differ in the Patriarchal, Mosaic, and Christian ages. Although the same basic principles underlie the requirements given in these dispensations, the specific demands are in many ways different. In addition to obvious differences in worship and other positive regulations, the divine requirements in these dispensations differ in the more complex area of moral commands (for instance, marriage and the related issues of divorce and polygamy).

Aside from having differences arising from the time factor, Bible books show vast differences in literary type. The manner of expression varies among these books, and the individual books often contain more than one literary type. Each of these styles of communication requires the application of corresponding principles of interpretation. This factor means that the Bible student must constantly adjust to the type of literature being interpreted.

Bible books are often labeled according to their prominent literary type. The Hebrews divided the Old Testament into three parts: Law or *Torah* (Gen. - Deut.), the Prophets or *Nabhaim* (Josh., Judg., I-II Sam., I-II Kings, Isa., Jer., Ezek., Hos., Joel, Amos, Obad., Jon., Mic., Nah., Hab., Zeph., Hag., Zech., Mal.) and the Writings or *Kethubhim* (Pss., Job, Prov., Ruth, Song of Sol., Eccles., Lam., Esther, Dan., Neh., I-II Chron.). Modern scholars usually divide the Old Testament into Law (Gen. - Deut.), History (Josh. - Esther), Poetry (Job - Song of Sol.), and Prophecy (Isa. - Mal.) and the New Testament into the Gospel accounts (Matt. - John), History (Acts), the Epistles (Rom. - Jude) and Prophecy (Rev.). Of course, this classification is general, since many of the books combine these types of writing.

Historical narrative is one of the most common types of biblical literature. The literalness of this type of writing and the familiarity of all cultures with the story as a teaching method make the narrative style a favored reading for many Bible students. These factors also lend themselves to a more immediate grasp of the meaning of the text. However, caution should be exercised in the application of such passages. Historical accounts often do not pass judgment on the actions recorded. They merely record what has occurred. Whether the actions are right or wrong may be revealed in other passages, leaving it unnecessary to reiterate this judgment in the historical record.

The literary designation *law* is given to Bible writings having a significant amount of explicit legal pronouncements. Two clarifications should be noted in regard to the use of this label. First, the term is sometimes extended to include the Old Testament in general, so that even the poetry of the Psalms is referred to as "the law" (John 10:34; 15:25). Second, an explicit legal pronouncement such as "thou shalt not kill" is not the only biblical way of teaching that a particular course of action is binding as law. The Bible also authorizes and forbids by examples (I Pet. 2:21; I Cor. 10:11). As a literary designation, the word *law* merely describes the manner of expression employed.

The books of prophecy receive this designation because of the twofold purpose of the message contained in them. During the age in which they were delivered, these messages consisted in the pronouncement of the judgment of God upon men and a call for them to return to Him. Concerning the future, the messages contained statements to be fulfilled at the coming of the Messiah. In the process of delivering the revelation, the prophets often employed highly figurative language, a fact especially seen in such books as Ezekiel and Revelation.

The poetic books of the Bible contribute a unique facet to the literary diversity of the Bible. The ability of these writings to touch the emotional side of man is well known, a fact particularly evident in such books as Psalms and Job. However, we must not forget that this type of literature is instructional as well as motivational; God teaches through this medium while motivating men to follow Him. Also, the context of verses in these books is often unusually short, especially in the book of Proverbs. The synthesis of Bible teaching is particularly important if misapplication of this literature is to be avoided.

The epistles or letters of the New Testament contain several literary characteristics that are crucial regarding their interpretation. As to their original recipients, they are the most personal and localized of biblical writings. The cultural, religious, and historical background of the recipients deserves attention in the interpretation of the books. Also, what is generally called "context" is a critical factor in the exegesis of the passages in these letters.

Though these differences deserve the attention of the interpreter, they should not be unreasonably magnified. The principles conveyed throughout the Scriptures transcend barriers of time, culture, and language. The gospel itself is an "everlasting covenant" (Heb. 13:20) and is applicable to "all men everywhere" (Acts 17:30). Also, the remarkable unity of the Bible in spite of the differences between the books is one of the most powerful arguments for its inspiration.

Distribution of Subject Matter

The fact that the Bible contains all the needed information on any topic necessary for salvation is assuring to Christians. This information, however, is seldom found in a single location. The Bible was not written like an encyclopedia. This characteristic of the Scriptures can be frustrating to an anxious Bible student, who at times may wish that God had delivered a topically arranged revelation resembling a Bible dictionary or a book on systematic theology. Instead, God gave man a revelation in which the various aspects, modifications, and qualifications of a topic appear in numerous locations of the Bible. These facets are woven into the story of the redemptive plan. Rather than causing frustration, the completeness of the Bible in view of its historical perspective should evoke our fascination.

Why was the Bible written in this manner? A topical revelation from God might appear at first glance to have desirable advantages. Such a revelation would seem to be more convenient and more exhaustive yet less liable to the danger of misinterpretation. It also would eliminate the difficulties involved in synthesizing biblical information. While these qualities seem attractive, a comparison of this type quickly encounters major problems. A topically arranged revelation would entail critical weaknesses and would fail to adequately correspond to the nature of man.

Man is an emotional as well as an intellectual being. He is not a computer that merely stores and retrieves information; he needs motivation for the use of those facts. The purpose of a dictionary is to inform, not motivate. If the Bible had been written in topical form, it would not be the "living and powerful" Word (Heb. 4:12). The story, for instance, has an intriguing effect on readers. A Bible dictionary may contain the facts of the story of Joseph in Genesis 37 - 50, but it cannot create the effects produced by the story itself. It may relate the basic facts of Nathan's confrontation with David in II Samuel 12, but it cannot reproduce the feelings evoked by Nathan's parable. Also, the beauty of poetry and the vividness of figurative language find no place in the literalness of a reference book. Who could imagine a book on systematic theology having the rhetorical properties of the Psalms or the impact achieved through use of the hyperbole?

The Bible was given to impart knowledge to man. But this knowledge is practical rather than theoretical. Knowledge of spiritual truth without action is useless. Motivation is needed, and the manner in which the Bible was written corresponds to this need. God intends for man to have knowledge of the truth (I Tim. 2:4), but He does not intend for Christians to be mere collections of facts. He demands an intellectual and emotional response to His revelation: "You shall love the Lord your God with all your heart . . . with all your mind . . ." (Mark 12:30). In fact, some Bible books were written to the original recipients to evoke a particular emotional response. John wrote, "And these things we write to you that your joy may be full (I John 1:4). Paul wrote, "I perceive that the same epistle made you sorry . . ." (II Cor. 7:8).

The complexity of synthesizing biblical information—an alleged weakness of non-topical revelation—is actually a point of advantage. The effort required for this step in interpretation is conducive to spiritual growth and demonstrates a sincere desire to know the will of God. It is good for a man to be challenged by a revelation of this kind. Evidently, God wants man to expend more effort in finding His will than he uses in a book in which subjects are arranged alphabetically!

The nature of biblical revelation also has certain advantages regarding the Bible student's perception of individual topics. Its non-topical arrangement lessens the tendency to isolate subjects; its indication and emphasis of "weightier matters" (Matt. 23:23) shows that Bible subjects are not on the same level of significance. The relative importance among subjects in a topical reference book would be difficult to determine.

The Conciseness of Scripture

As a book for all nations since the time of its completion, the Bible is remarkably brief. One might expect a revelation of universal applicability to involve enormous length. Human law systems, in spite of explicit details of legislation, are subject to disputes in interpretation and are in constant need of revision. But God supplies us with all necessary truth in one volume. This characteristic is particularly true of the New Testament—an amazingly concise covenant in view of its universal application.

A primary reason the Bible can retain both the properties of comprehensiveness and conciseness is that it makes frequent use of *principles*. Conveyed by direct statements, examples of behavior and even figurative discourses, these general principles of righteousness transcend barriers of time, language, and nationality. This is why the Mosaic covenant—a law system given specifically to Israel for a limited time—applies in principle to all nations of every age. The New Testament, however, is not merely a set of general principles; it contains specific details of legislation. Qualifications of bishops (I Tim. 3:1-7), steps in resolving conflict (Matt. 18:15-17), and the observance of the Lord's Supper (Matt. 26:26-29) are specific requirements in any age. While the two covenants differ markedly in positive legislation, certain fundamental principles inhere in each.

In addition to the expedient value of the use of principles, a more fundamental rationale is behind the conciseness of the Bible. God's basic reason for creating the world was to provide man the opportunity of choosing his eternal destiny. This purpose was the governing factor in how He created the world and how He revealed Himself to man. Since He requires that men serve Him out of love, God gave man free will and has provided the ideal environment for its exercise. The world contains elements that challenge the will without stifling it; the revelation of God both in nature and in the Scriptures is neither too intense so that man is overwhelmed nor too vague so that man cannot discover Him. A perfect balance in creation and revelation preserves the opportunity for the proper exercise of the will.

The degree of explicitness in the Bible corresponds to this purpose. When men cry out for a more explicit revelation from God, they ask for something that would counteract the very reason for creation. A Bible with explicit details on every phase of man's existence would infringe upon the exercise of the will and would stifle the growth process of Bible study. Every obligation would be specified in minute, personal aspects of application. Taken to its logical end, this philosophy of revelation would necessitate each person's having a different Bible. This Bible would contain every action of the person's life—before it occurred. Such an enormous "personalized Bible" would be practically useless, leaving no time for the practice of the responsibilities so explicitly stated in its pages.

Wise parents do not explain in explicit terms every phase of a child's responsibilities. They give the child room to figure out some matters on his own. As our all-wise Father, God has not specified every facet of the life He requires us to live. He has revealed these facets, but some of them can be discovered only through diligent, persistent study. He expects us to figure out some things by fitting together the information given us in the Scriptures.

2

Explanation of the Principle

Analogies

A study of the nature of God often begins with an analysis of His individual attributes. Given the premise that the Supreme Being is infinite in every attribute, defining the attributes in general terms is relatively easy. For instance, we say that God is omnipotent (all-powerful) and omniscient (all-knowing). After the basic meaning of each attribute is determined, however, significant broader questions present themselves. How can these attributes, existing together in Deity, form a logically consistent whole? What relationships exist between the individual attributes? How is each attribute to be defined in its relationship to other attributes?

The attribute of omnipotence means that God is all-powerful. In Jesus' words, "With God all things are possible" (Matt. 19:26). But "all things" in this verse is not unqualified; it refers to a definite category the boundaries of which are established by moral and logical qualifications. Although He is omnipotent, it is "impossible for God to lie" (Heb. 6:18). The attribute of holiness in God qualifies His omnipotence so that He "cannot lie" (Titus 1:2). Also, the attributes of justice and goodness in God qualify omnipotence so that, properly understood, this attribute should produce both awe and gratitude in man.

If political power unchecked by virtue is a frightening thought, the idea of a God of raw, unqualified power is horrifying indeed. Such arbitrary omnipotence could conceivably reward the ungodly in heaven and punish the righteous in hell. Thankfully for us, God is perfectly loving and just as well as infinite in power.

Calvin's view of the nature of God is a prime example of the failure to recognize the qualifying relationship between God's attributes. His overemphasis on the sovereignty of God occurred at the expense of His justice and goodness. From his belief that Paul attributed "supreme sovereignty to the wrath and power of God,"[1] Calvin concluded, "everything which he wills must be held to be righteous by the mere fact of his willing it."[2] In this assertion Calvin subscribes to the first alternative in the proposed dilemma of Plato's *Euthyphro*:[3] Are things good because God approves of them or does God approve of things because they are good? Realizing the implications of this position, Calvin added that he gave no countenance to the "fiction of absolute power."[4] However, this disclaimer is inconsistent with his assertion that righteousness is determined merely by God's will. The sovereignty of God receives a status in the *Institutes* that no other attributes enjoy. His treatment of the attributes of God suggests a hierarchy in which the sovereignty of God is supreme and all other attributes are subservient. In Calvin's theology, the sovereignty of God governs all other attributes, but the other attributes are not permitted to qualify (and thus correctly define) His sovereign power.

A reciprocal qualification exists between the divine attributes of benevolence and justice. Though God in His love both de-

[1]John Calvin, *Institutes of the Christian Religion,* Henry Beveridge, trans. (Grand Rapids, MI: William B. Eerdmans Publishing Company, 1983 reprint), Vol. 2, p. 226.

[2]*Ibid.,* p. 227.

[3]Plato, "Euthyphro," *The Last Days of Socrates,* Hugh Tredennick, trans. (Baltimore, MD: Penguin Books Incorporated, 1954) p. 31.

[4]Calvin, *Institutes,* Vol. 2, p. 227.

sires and makes provisions for the salvation of all men (I Tim. 2:4; Titus 2:11), His justice will not allow the impenitent to enter heaven (I Cor. 6:9-10). In this sense, His justice qualifies His benevolence. Failure to recognize this qualification creates a distorted view of God, resulting in a permissive and tolerant view of love. The loving mercy of God may in a sense be said to qualify the attribute of justice. Bare justice provides no room for the opportunity of repentance and pardon; it simply requires that transgressions be punished. This qualification is seen in that

> He has not dealt with us according to our sins, nor punished us according to our iniquities. For as the heavens are high above the earth, so great is His mercy toward those who fear Him (Ps. 103:10-11).

To speak of the nature of God in this manner, however, is to invite a further legitimate question about even engaging in such a discussion. Since God is infinite in all His attributes and since the word *qualify* means "to limit," how can these attributes be qualified? Obviously, the word is used accommodatively in this connection. In our inability to fully comprehend the nature of God, we create in our minds a tension between certain attributes of God. This difficulty arises from viewing the attributes of God in isolation. Such an atomistic approach is destined for confusion because the meaning and perfection of each attribute depends on its relationship to the other attributes. In other words, part of the perfection of God's power lies in the fact that it is "qualified" by His goodness, justice, and wisdom. These attributes are so connected that this interrelationship is an essential property of each attribute. The attributes of God should be studied as a logically consistent whole, not as characteristics existing independently of this relationship.

Since the will of God as revealed in His word is an expression of His nature, this analogy furnishes a general framework for interpreting qualifications in Scripture. The point at which one biblical principle ends and another begins its application has its origin in the nature of God.

The principle of qualification is also a part of God's creation. The laws and forces of nature work in unison to bring about the purposes of the Creator, complementing and at times qualifying one another. This relationship is such an important part of creation that

> through all nature, the higher law dominates the lower. Human volition throws the stone in opposition to gravitation. Vegetable life builds the tree in opposition to gravity, and to those chemical forces, which, when life departs, fulfill the old decree, "earth to earth, and dust to dust." Man's higher power continually directs and modifies natural forces. The law of miracles, the power of God, is higher than all else, and may dominate all else; and this would be but one of the great class of facts.[5]

Upon graduating from using a bottle to drinking out of a glass, a young child soon discovers that this new utensil cannot be turned upside down at will. However, a few years later in science class he learns that he can momentarily "cheat" the law of gravity by rapidly swinging a glass or a pail of water in a circular motion. In this unique circumstance, the principle of centrifugal force qualifies the law of gravity. Properly understood, the law of gravity is a fundamental principle that is qualified by other forces present in nature.

Recognition of the principle of qualification at work in nature is a major reason for the rapid progress of civilization in the last century. Working together in marvelous unity, the interrelationship of forces in nature provides a fascinating arena of possibilities.

Miracles bear a different relationship to the laws of nature. Since these interventions originate from a source beyond nature, they are not qualifications of natural processes in the sense mentioned above. During supernatural activity, certain

[5]Harvey W. Everest, *The Divine Demonstration: A Textbook of Christian Evidences* (Nashville, TN: Gospel Advocate Company, 1972), p. 23.

laws of nature are actually suspended. It is better therefore to refer to miracles as suspensions, rather than qualifications, of the laws of nature.

More important to the analogy is Harvey W. Everest's observation of gradation of forces in creation in which the higher law overrules the lower. This distinction finds an important parallel in interpretation, since the question of higher/lower laws is a crucial issue in the application of biblical principles.

Aside from these more abstract analogies, the principle of qualification in Scripture is analogous to everyday sets of instruction. Parental rules are usually general guidelines that are qualified by instructions and principles in the total amount of information conveyed to the child. A child who is expected to clean his room at certain times is not held responsible for omitting this responsibility in cases of sickness or family emergency. These extenuating circumstances qualify the normal duty required by the instructions. Of course, just what these circumstances include may be vague in the mind of the child. Ideally, the child recognizes the legitimate circumstances (which are determined by more fundamental concerns of the family) by information previously given by the parents. Still, parental instructions illustrate the use of the principle of qualification as a convenient as well as necessary part of child rearing.

Employees are also involved in interpreting qualifying information given to them. They are expected to recognize qualifications of particular instructions by fitting those instructions into the broader programs and goals of the company.

The presence of the principle of qualification in these familiar areas should prevent our thinking that this subject is overly complex. Qualification is inherent in most discourse and is not peculiar to the Scriptures.

Synthesizing Biblical Material

Interpreting the Bible involves examining its contents in various levels of size. The study of individual words (which may include an analysis of the units of meaning comprising the

words themselves) must be given an adequate degree of attention. This area of interpretation, known as *lexicology*, is primarily concerned with arriving at the meaning of words. The
study of the function of the individual words in relationship to
other words in the sentence is known as *syntax*. This aspect of
interpretation focuses on grammatical relationships and seeks
to determine the meaning of the sentence. The general thought
expressed by a succession of sentences (which also governs the
direction of those sentences) is usually referred to as the context. Linguists refer to this crucial phase of interpretation as
discourse analysis.[6] In the broader setting of the book in which
it appears, a given context serves as a thought unit that con-
tributes to the overall purpose and theme of the particular
book. Also involved in the contents of the book is the historical-
cultural context which is concerned with historical and cultural
aspects that are relevant to interpretation.

Important as these areas of interpretation are, the efforts
given to them are risky if a further phase is not pursued: the
synthesis of all related biblical information, perhaps more commonly known as interpreting the Bible as a whole. The various

[6]Silva refers to this field of study as a "rather young" discipline (*God,
Language, and Scripture*, Zondervan, 1990, p. 119). While the formal study
of this aspect of interpretation in terms of language in general may be
relatively new, the suggestion that modern linguistics has uncovered a previously unrecognized key in biblical interpretation is absurd. Serious Bible
students have always consulted the context to determine the meaning of a
word, phrase, or sentence. Also, several writers stressed the importance of
context prior to the alleged discovery of linguists. Louis Berkhof wrote, "In
the study of separate words, the most important question is not that of their
etymological meaning, nor even that of the various significations which they
gradually acquired. The essential point is that of their particular sense in the
connection in which they occur" (*Principles of Biblical Interpretation*, Baker,
1950, p. 74). Terry (*Biblical Hermeneutics*, Zondervan, p. 210) and Ramm
(*Protestant Biblical Interpretation*, Baker, pp. 139-140) also emphasized the
primacy of context in interpretation. In the tradition of Barr and others,
Silva is reacting to theologians whose negligence of the context has resulted
in what he appropriately calls "overinterpretation." While the warning
linguists have sounded remains timely and legitimate, it is certainly not a
new one.

facets of a topic, often found in several distant passages, must be correctly fitted together before the final stage—the application of biblical principles to life—can be entered. This process requires careful research and honest reasoning, since an omitted relevant text or a significant misconstrued passage will adversely affect the final conclusions drawn by the interpreter. The fact that the Bible must be studied in this manner is a constant challenge, since all the information on a topic is rarely found in one verse.

Interpreting the Bible as a whole means that the entirety of Scripture is the total context for the interpretation of any of its parts. Any individual passage must be interpreted considering this total context. A verse must be viewed in relationship to the rest of Scripture—an exercise traditionally called "the analogy of faith." As Ramm observed, "The Bible is not a string of verses like a string of beads, but a web of meaning."[7] He later states that

> the context of any verse is the entire Scripture. This is what is meant by "Scripture interprets Scripture" . . . This is a principle difficult to manage, but it does say procedurally or programmatically that the "universe of discourse," the "locale," the "habitat" of any passage of Scripture is the total Scripture. It sets the general mood, gives the general perspective, governs the fundamental assumptions, or sets the possible limits of meaning for the interpreter of Holy Scripture.[8]

The necessity of synthesizing biblical passages is seen in that

> the principal subjects treated in the Scriptures are presented to us more or less piecemeal, being scattered over its pages and made known under various aspects, some clearly and fully, others more remotely and tersely: in different connections and with different accompaniments

---

[7]Bernard Ramm, *Protestant Biblical Interpretation: A Textbook of Hermeneutics* (Grand Rapids, MI: Baker Book House, 1970), p. 37.

[8]*Ibid.,* p. 37.

in the several passages where they occur. This was designed by God in His manifold wisdom to make us search His Word. It is evident that if we are to apprehend His fully made known mind on any particular subject we must collect and collate all passages in which it is adverted to, or in which a similar thought or sentiment is expressed; and by this method we may be assured that if we conduct our investigation in a right spirit, and with diligence and perseverance, we shall arrive at a clear knowledge of His revealed will. The Bible is somewhat like a mosaic, whose fragments are scattered here and there through the Word, and those fragments have to be gathered by us and carefully fitted together if we are to obtain the complete picture of any one of its innumerable objects. There are many places in the Scriptures which can be understood only by the explanations and amplifications furnished by other passages.[9]

This interrelationship of Bible verses means that other passages can have a significant effect on the interpretation of a verse. One of these effects is *amplification.* Complementary verses often amplify a passage by providing an example or illustration of the principle being stated in the passage. For instance, Solomon's proverb, "The way of the unfaithful is hard" (Prov. 13:15), is powerfully and repeatedly illustrated in the Scriptures, especially in the Old Testament. The story of Saul (I Sam. 10-31), a man who by his own admission "played the fool" (I Sam. 26:21), vividly illustrates the digressive course of one who departs from God. In fact, much of the Bible restates in different forms the same basic principles. If these principles had been delivered to man in concise abstract form, the Bible would be a brief volume indeed. But God supplements the principles stated in bare conceptual form with amplifying material, providing an adequate amount of both abstract and concrete teaching.

[9]Arthur W. Pink, *Interpretation of the Scriptures* (Grand Rapids, MI: Baker Book House, 1972), pp. 42-43.

Another effect that relevant passages have on a verse is *clarification.* Supplemental material in the Bible may clarify a verse in question by explaining its meaning, adding key details, or identifying its fulfillment. The book of II Thessalonians appears to have been written to correct a misapprehension about the previous epistle. From Paul's description of the second coming in I Thessalonians 4:13 - 5:3, particularly, "We which are alive and remain . . ." (v. 17), some Thessalonians had evidently concluded that Christ would return in their lifetime. Paul clarifies this issue in the second epistle by declaring, ". . . That day will not come unless the falling away comes first . . ." (II Thess. 2:3). Abraham's statement concerning Isaac, "The lad and I will go yonder and worship, and we will come back to you" (Gen. 22:5), is clarified by the details supplied in a New Testament passage: "By faith Abraham, when he was tested, offered up Isaac . . . accounting that God was able to raise him up, even from the dead . . ." (Heb. 11:17, 19).

Peter identified the fulfillment of Joel 2:28-32 in saying "this is what was spoken by the prophet Joel" (Acts 2:16); Jesus identified the Elijah of Malachi's prophecy (Mal. 4:5) by saying of John the Baptist, "He is Elijah who is to come" (Matt. 11:14). Scripture thus clarifies Scripture, rendering the Bible a self-interpreting book.

Supplemental passages also may have a *modifying* effect on a given verse. In the original legislation delivered while the Israelites were in Egypt, the Passover was to be observed on the fourteenth day of the first month (Exod. 12:2-6). However, in specified circumstances the Passover could be observed on the fourteenth day of the second month (Num. 9:9-14). Making provisions for the observance of the Passover in these special circumstances, the passage in Numbers modified the original legislation given in Egypt.

When one biblical passage limits or restricts another passage, the effect is called *qualification.* A familiar example of this principle occurs in the account of Jesus' temptation in the wilderness. After setting Him on the pinnacle of the temple, the devil challenged Jesus:

> If you are the Son of God, throw yourself down. For it is written: "He shall give His angels charge concerning you," and, "In their hands they shall bear you up, lest you dash your foot against a stone" (Matt. 4:6).

In this phase of the temptation, Satan appealed to the Scriptures. But his citation of Psalm 91:11-12 was misapplied. The providential care promised in this passage did not extend to cases of deliberate attempts to test the faithfulness of God to this promise. In response to Satan's challenge, Jesus cited Deuteronomy 6:16, "You shall not tempt the Lord your God," as a qualification of the promise of providential care. The protection promised in the Psalms passage must be viewed considering biblical teaching on human responsibility. This obvious example of "twisting" the Scriptures (II Pet. 3:16) illustrates the need for examining the hermeneutical relationship called qualification.

Old Testament teaching on the taking of human life is a case of qualification with significant consequences for modern times. The Decalogue warned, "You shall not murder" (Exod. 20:13), yet the law also required the death penalty (Exod. 21:12-17; Lev. 20:1-21). In fact, divine authorization for capital punishment was given before Moses: "Whoever sheds man's blood, by man his blood will be shed; for in the image of God He made man" (Gen. 9:6). Critics of the Bible allege that the Scriptures are contradictory in both commanding and forbidding the taking of human life.

A common approach to reconciling these passages emphasizes the distinction between the English words *kill* and *murder*. The general word *kill* means "to deprive of life; put to death; cause the death of,"[10] while the more specific word *murder* means "to kill (a human being) unlawfully and with

[10]*Webster's Third New International Dictionary* (Chicago: Encyclopedia Britannica, Incorporated, 1981), Vol. II, p. 1242.

premeditated malice."[11] Thus "*kill* merely states the fact" while "*murder* implies motive and usually premeditation in a criminal human act."[12] Archer argues that this same distinction exists in Hebrew:

> . . . Much confusion has arisen from the misleading translation of Exodus 20:13 that occurs in most English versions. The Hebrew original uses a specific word for murder (*rasah*) in the sixth commandment and should be rendered "You shall not murder" (NASB). This is no prohibition against capital punishment for capital crimes, since it is not a general term for the taking of life, such as our English word "kill" implies.[13]

An examination of Hebrew words and phrases denoting the taking of life, however, reveals the weakness of this argument. *Rasah* itself is used of one who "kills (*rasah*) his neighbor unintentionally" (Deut. 19:4). Also, the word *harag* is used to refer both to killing with malicious intent (Gen. 12:12; Judg. 9:24) and killing in capital punishment (Deut. 13:9; Lev. 20:16). The phrase "shed blood" (*shapak dam*) is used in both senses in Genesis 9:6. Even if Archer's case on *rasah* were successful, the difficulty would remain in these passages. Rather than trying to solve the alleged discrepancy on the basis of linguistic nuances, one should consult qualifying information from the overall context of the Scriptures.

At least four categories of taking human life emerge from Old Testament teaching: (1) the intentional, malicious taking of human life (Num. 35:20-21); (2) the unpremeditated taking of human life, perhaps from a fight (Num. 35:22-23); (3) the accidental causing of death (Deut. 19:4-6); (4) the intentional infliction of death as a deserved form of punishment, either by direct intervention of God (Lev. 10:1-2) or through human agency (Deut. 21:22). The killing involved in the first type is the act prohibited in the Decalogue. The other three types

---

[11] *Webster's Third New International Dictionary*, p. 1488.

[12] *Ibid.*, p. 1242.

[13] Gleason L. Archer, *Encyclopedia of Bible Difficulties* (Grand Rapids, MI: Zondervan Publishing House, Regency Reference Library, 1982), p. 121.

qualify the application of this prohibition. Also, the second and third types qualify the application of the death penalty, since this punishment was not ordered in cases of unpremeditated or accidental killing.

Types of Qualifications

Qualifying considerations occur in various forms, differing in their degree of explicitness and in their proximity to the qualified statements. Beginning with factors within the verse itself, this limiting effect may be accomplished in the following manners:

1. *Words or phrases in a passage that restrict the meaning and application of the statement in question.* The phrases "except for sexual immorality" (Matt. 19:9), "yet I certainly did not mean" (I Cor. 5:10), and " 'Conscience', I say, not your own" (I Cor. 10:29) are explicit qualifications that are negative in force, indicating what the meaning of the teaching *is not.* Such explicit qualifications are rare in Scripture. If after every instruction in the Bible God had explained what the passage does not mean, the cumbersome list of endless qualifications would cause the reader to lose the real point of discussion.

2. *The immediate context or thought flow in which the statement occurs.* The limitations established by the thought setting of a verse must be recognized if the teaching is to be correctly applied. For instance, Solomon's often misconstrued statement, "The dead know nothing" (Eccles. 9:5), is restricted by the context to knowledge of earthly affairs (vv. 1-10). The interpretation of a verse in its immediate context is a foundational step in hermeneutics, furnishing a precedent for how the procedure should be handled in larger contexts of Scripture. The principles of interpreting a verse in the total context of Scripture are basically the same as those involved in interpreting a statement in its immediate context.

3. *The overall purpose and theme of the book in which the verse appears.* The purpose of Hebrews, for example, is to establish and to show the implications of its summary verse: "For the priesthood being changed, of necessity there is also a change of the law" (Heb. 7:12). Just as a verse must be interpreted in view of its immediate context, this immediate context must be viewed in relation to the basic direction of the book in which it occurs.

4. *The relative aspects of the culture in which the biblical writing was originally delivered.* Jesus' command to "wash one another's feet" (John 13:14) and Paul's instruction to "greet one another with a holy kiss" (Rom. 16:16) are qualified by cultural considerations. Interpretation in such matters involves separating culturally bound instructions from the permanent principles they exemplify.

5. *The temporal factors associated with the particular age in which the instruction was given.* "Make yourself an ark of gopherwood" (Gen. 6:14) is limited in application to Noah because of his peculiar historical situation. Noah's response to this instruction, however, was a demonstration of the permanent principle of faith (Heb. 11:7).

6. *A change in divine covenants.* In one respect, such a transition amounts to the annulment, not the mere qualification, of previously given legislation. The revocation of animal sacrifices by the law of Christ illustrates this fact. In another respect, a later covenant qualifies the previous one, since some principles in the earlier covenant remain in force in the new law.

7. *Circumstantial considerations in terms of the limits of physical possibility and in view of practical expedience.* God does not require the impossible of man. If a man is literally unable to perform a duty, God does not hold him responsible. The principle of human inability resulting from physical limitations qualifies corresponding obliga-

tions. Also, some divine commands are restricted in application because of considerations of expedience. Though God had given man the institution of marriage, Jeremiah was forbidden to marry because of the impending dangers families would face (Jer. 16:1-4).

8. *Statements in the remote context that limit the application of a verse.* This relationship may be recognized when two passages are compared and an unqualified interpretation of both yields a contradiction. On a surface level, the two statements appear to conflict.

9. *Authorized actions of biblical characters that constitute exemptions from general commands.* Some qualifications occur in the form of examples found in the remote context. Care in interpretation is necessary at this point, since some recorded actions in the Bible are without divine approval.

10. *An overriding principle that takes precedence over a biblical requirement in cases of apparent conflict.* The qualifying factor in this circumstance is the relative primacy of the overriding principle. This factor determines which course of action is to be pursued in alleged moral dilemmas.

The first five of these types are involved in the exegesis of individual passages from considerations within the books in which they occur. Though each of these is a critical matter of interpretation, this study will focus on the last five types. These latter types involve a consideration of qualifying information found outside the confines of the immediate setting of the book. The first five emphasize the interpretation of individual verses; the last five stress the relationship between verses as they occur in the broader context of the Bible as a whole. This connection is a matter of implication, since most biblical qualifications are not explicit. The type of qualification being considered in this study involves the identification of implied qualifications through a synthesis of biblical material found in the remote context.

When God issues a command, He has in view a definite realm of application. The boundaries of that realm must be identified if the precept is to be correctly applied. By implied qualifications, the Bible establishes these boundaries. Just as the immediately surrounding context of a verse may qualify its meaning, this distant material may qualify the command in question. These qualifications delineate the point at which one biblical principle ends and another begins. The principle of qualification involves a definitional aspect in that it defines the category or realm in which a biblical mandate applies.

Areas Which Must Deal With the Principle

Though the principle of qualification is primarily a hermeneutical issue, it is also a critical consideration in other fields of study. The basic premises, emphases, and views of specialists in these areas is to a large extent determined by how they synthesize biblical material. But since these branches of study are areas of the Christian life, the problems and issues involved in the study of the principle of qualification should be the concern of every Christian. Though a study of this type may seem purely theoretical, a consideration of its connection to these areas reveals its practicality as well as its importance.

The qualification of moral duties is a fundamental issue in the study of ethics. The biblical answer to ethical questions is not always stated in explicit terms. Often two or more biblical principles seem relevant (or even applicable) to the situation in question. When the requirements of two different passages cannot both be satisfied in a given situation (although both of them appear to apply to the situation), a choice must be made. The Christian at this juncture must determine the point at which the application of one biblical principle ends and the application of another begins. Which principle qualifies and which is qualified? The apparent tension between biblical principles is seen in as commonplace an occurrence as a Christian who unintentionally orders in a restaurant more food than he can temperately eat. If he eats the remaining food, he transgresses the biblical principle of self-control; if he does not, he appears to violate stewardship principles. Has he led himself into a no-win situation? Which biblical principle prevails in this situation? Is there a third alternative or some other way to resolve the apparent conflict?

To attempt to deal with these questions at this point would be premature. At this stage, the example above shows the reality of such choices in everyday life and the need for determining biblical guidelines for making proper decisions. A quick, easy answer is rarely available in such situations. The situation may be one which we have not previously encountered, and this factor adds to the complexity of the case. If judgment may be suspended, time will be afforded to reflect on the matter before making a decision. An extended period of time in making ethical decisions allows one to study relevant biblical material, consult the advice of godly and wise Christians, and pray to God for wisdom (James 1:5). But when no such suspension of judgment is possible, a choice must be made based on prior knowledge. Because of the regularity of such decisions, it is wise to give attention to the study of biblical qualification in the realm of ethics. Though it is impossible to foresee every conceivable situation, knowledge of basic biblical principles provides the general framework necessary for ethical decisions. Applied consistently, these principles give direction in specific cases. They also establish a solid foundation against changing ethical theories and trends in society.

Of course, it would be naive to think that pure mechanical knowledge of these principles guarantees right behavior. This Socratic myth continues to live through the current emphasis on education as the answer to societal ills such as crime, poverty, drug abuse, and promiscuity. But while knowledge of right and wrong is necessary to right behavior, such knowledge does not always insure proper moral decisions. The missing element in humanistic approaches to ethics is the primacy of free will in human actions. Because of the fact of free will and the intensity of the emotions, one who has knowledge of right and wrong may choose the wrong path. Even a conscientious, knowledgeable person may choose to sin because of the unexpected pressures of temptation. Peter boasted that he would never deny the Lord only to contradict his claim hours later (Luke 22:33-34; Matt. 26:69-75). It is possible to "sin willfully after we have received the knowledge of the truth" (Heb. 10:26). While this factor in human behavior cannot be ignored, a legitimate need remains for determining the biblical criteria for making decisions in difficult moral issues.

The field of systematic theology also addresses numerous subjects affected by the principle of qualification. The totality of Bible teaching on a topic may be obtained only through the synthesis of its different aspects. This step in interpretation is critical. Faulty reasoning in this process leads to doctrines not found in Scripture. This stage is the point at which many Bible-believing people part company with each other, since they disagree as to how to view the Bible as a whole. Much division exists because of different applications of the principle of qualification.

The area of doctrine is affected in at least three ways by the principle of qualification. One is the identification of portions of Scripture that are no longer applicable. Several important questions must be dealt with to make this determination. Was the passage in question qualified by a change in the covenants? Is it limited in application because of cultural considerations? Are the demands of the passage confined to a special period of divine activity?

Another point of concern is the distinction between obligatory matters and optional matters. A failure to consider qualifying information may result in the over-application of a biblical command. On the other hand, the same error can lead to an over-extension of the concept of liberty in the New Testament.

Connected with the question of essentials and nonessentials is the relative degree of emphasis to be given to the various items of biblical doctrine. Even when all matters of biblical doctrine have been identified, it is evident that not all of them receive the same emphasis in Scripture. Some principles are more basic and foundational than others; Jesus spoke of "the weightier matters of the law" (Matt. 23:23). An understanding of this proportional emphasis in Scripture is vital for several reasons.

First, it enables spiritual leaders to weigh the urgency of biblically related issues. Out of the enormous number of such issues presenting themselves, which ones should be given the most attention? A general framework is needed for determining the relative importance of these issues.

Second, recognition of this aspect of Scripture is a safeguard against extremism in doctrine. Radical doctrines are not so much the result of denying biblical principles as they are the result of getting them out of proportion.

Third, an understanding of this point enables one to detect the underlying issue in many religious disagreements. A surprising number of disputes arise, not because the disputants each deny the principle asserted by the other, but because they disagree about the amount of emphasis that should be given to it. Sadly, this underlying disagreement often goes unnoticed, especially by the disputants.

The study of the principle of qualification also has a place in apologetics. As a part of synthesizing biblical passages, the resolving of alleged discrepancies in the Bible is often a simple matter of recognizing an implied qualification. However, when scriptural statements are invariably taken as unqualified assertions, a conflict is created in the mind of the interpreter. In fact, any number of discrepancies can be imagined if important qualifications from the immediate context or from the entire context of the Bible are ignored.

The fundamental distinction to be made is the difference between qualification and contradiction. The law of contradiction states that a proposition cannot be both true and false at the same time and in the same sense. When two statements contradict each other, one must be true and the other false. If one of the propositions is true, the other must be false, and if one of the propositions is false, the other must be true. It is impossible for both statements to be true or for both statements to be false. But it is essential that the two propositions have an identical point of reference. The two statements must make contradictory assertions about precisely the same thing.

The propositions, "All men are equal" and "Some men are not equal," are contradictory only if the word *equal* has the same meaning in both statements. The statements, "I have seen God" (Gen. 32:30) and "No one has seen God at any time" (John 1:18) would be contradictory only if "seeing God" had the same meaning in both verses. In this case, Jacob's experience was the witnessing of a physical manifestation of God called a theophany; John's passage refers to seeing the very essence of God—an impossible feat for human eyes (I Tim. 6:16). Qualification, on the other hand, is the limiting or restricting of one statement by another, and this is the relationship that exists between these verses. A qualification is not a categorical denial of a statement. It simply sets the statement in perspective by supplying additional facets of information about the subject under consideration.

3

Evaluation of
Common Approaches

As serious Bible study quickly reveals, the harmonizing of biblical passages is a necessary and regular part of interpretation. When an impasse is reached in Bible study, a solution must be derived before application of the biblical principles is made. The following approaches are some common faulty methods that attempt to harmonize apparent tension between Bible verses. Obviously, the examination of any of these methods could be a volume in itself. What is presented here is a brief description of each approach and the key problems connected with it. In addition, sources for further research are included.

The Rejection of Seeking Solutions

The most extreme way of dealing with perceived tension between biblical principles is to claim that the Bible contradicts itself. This approach rejects the search for solutions on the premise that no such solutions exist. Aside from the evidence of the divine inspiration of the Bible and the adequate transmission of its text—evidence so compelling as to rule out the possibility of a fallible Bible[1]—some other factors make the

[1] For a discussion of this evidence, the following works are suggested: Edward J. Young, *Thy Word is Truth* (Grand Rapids, MI: William B. Eerdmans Publishing Company, 1957); Clark H. Pinnock, *A Defense of Biblical Infallibility* (Phillipsburg, NJ: Presbyterian and Reformed Publishing Company,

charge of contradiction inadmissible. Of these factors, a consideration frequently ignored by those making the charge is the peculiar manner of expression, computation, and recording found in the Bible. To demand that people in a distant ancient culture speak in accord with modern conventional standards of language is extremely unfair, yet this is precisely the conformity expected by critics of the Bible. Biblical language does not contradict itself. But it does differ vastly from the manner of speaking commonly used today. Another important consideration is the evident divine intention to provide a revelation suitable for challenging the exercise of man's free will. As in nature, the difficulties in the Bible are designed to stimulate man to respond freely in loving obedience to the Creator.

A less extreme version of this approach is the rejection of (sufficiently attested) verses or even whole books of the 66-book canon of Scripture. Marcion, a second century writer branded by Tertullian and others as a heretic, accepted Luke alone out of the four gospel accounts and only ten of Paul's epistles, rejecting the rest of the New Testament books.[2] Luther's well-known assessment of the epistle of James as *ein rechte stroern Epistel*[3], "a right strawy epistle," in the first edition of his German New Testament (1522) was based on the belief that James "contradicts Paul and all Scripture"[4] on the relation of works and faith. Luther held that it is impossible to reconcile James and other New Testament writers, especially Paul, on

1967); *The Inspiration and Authority of the Bible: The 1971 Harding Graduate School of Religion Lectureship* (Nashville, TN: Gospel Advocate Company, 1971); *The Spiritual Sword* (Memphis, TN: Getwell Church of Christ), January 1970.

[2]Tertullian "The Five Books Against Marcion," *The Ante-Nicene Fathers*, Alexander Roberts and James Donaldson, eds. (Grand Rapids, MI: William B. Eerdmans Publishing Company, 1980 reprint), Vol. 3, pp. 269-275.

[3]James Hardy Ropes, *The International Critical Commentary: A Critical and Exegetical Commentary on the Epistle of St. James* (Edinburg: T. & T. Clark, 1978), p. 106.

[4]John Dillenberger, ed., *Martin Luther: Selections From His Writings* (Gorden City, NY: Anchor Books, 1961), p. 36.

this subject. Luther's distaste for the Catholic system of works-righteousness colored his interpretation, preventing him from seeing the harmony between James and other New Testament writers. While man is not saved by meritorious works (Eph. 2:8-9), he must demonstrate faith in works of obedience (James 2:14-26).

Others have rejected the search for logical solutions to apparent conflicts in Scripture because of the conviction that such an intellectually mechanical approach to the Bible is incompatible with a heart-felt practice of religion. The concern is that an emphasis on reason in Christianity robs man of emotional involvement in religion. Such an impersonal approach is considered cold and lifeless, preventing a personal relationship with Christ. This concern is known in popular terms as the struggle between "the head and the heart" and is an aspect of theological discussions regarding the relationship of faith and reason. It has been expressed in various forms since the time of Aquinas, the most famous leader in the medieval movement known as *scholasticism*.[5] His approach focused on logical deduction, a fact especially evident in his five proofs for the existence of God. Because this focus was perceived as an overemphasis of the role of the intellect in religion, some reactions to scholasticism abandoned the role of reason in Christianity altogether. This response sometimes appeared in the form of mysticism, as in Johannes Eckhart's (1260-1327) attempt to present Christianity as a religion of deep feelings rather than logical proof.[6]

Another form of this reaction became known as *fideism*, the view that Christianity is incapable of being logically proved and must be accepted by faith, not evidence. This movement culminated in the writings of nineteenth century Danish philosopher Soren Kierkegaard, whose views have become increasingly influential in modern Western Protestantism. Rejecting

[5]Samuel Enoch Stumpf, *Philosophy: History and Problems* (New York: McGraw-Hill Book Company, 1983), p. 169.
[6]*Ibid.*, p. 191.

attempts to prove the claims of Scripture, Kierkegaard regarded faith as an emotional engagement rather than an intellectual activity. He held that proving God's existence is impossible, since

> at the very outset, in beginning my proof, I would have
> presupposed it, not as doubtful but as certain (a presupposition is never doubtful, for the very reason that it is a
> presupposition), since otherwise I would not begin . . .[7]

For Kierkegaard, passion, not reason, is the essence of faith. In fact, he claims that "deepest down in the heart of piety lurks the mad caprice which knows that it has itself produced the God."[8] In describing the process by which faith is attained, Kierkegaard introduced a word which has since become commonplace in Protestant discussions of faith: leap.[9] Belief in God, then, is a "leap" of faith, a passionate, personal experience, not a conclusion from logical argumentation. Briefly stated, "faith begins precisely there where thinking leaves off."[10] Faith is "the highest passion in a man,"[11] but it is not "an act of the will."[12]

In regard to harmonizing seeming tensions between biblical statements, Kierkegaard's approach finds expression in his concept of the paradox. Perhaps his most famous illustration of this concept is Abraham's attempted sacrifice of Isaac in Genesis 22. Abraham is known as a great example of faith even though his actions were not only unjustified by reason but were also contrary to it. Accordingly, "Abraham enjoys honor and glory as the father of faith, whereas he ought to be prosecuted and convicted of murder."[13] Kierkegaard's example of

---

[7]Soren Kierkegaard, *Philosophical Fragments* (Princeton, NJ: Princeton University Press, 1962), p. 49.

[8]*Ibid.*, p. 46.

[9]*Ibid.*, p. 53.

[10]Soren Kierkegaard, *Fear and Trembling and the Sickness Unto Death*, Walter Lowrie, trans. (Garden City, NY: Doubleday & Company, 1954), p. 64.

[11]*Ibid.*, p. 131.

[12]Kierkegaard, *Philosophical Fragments*, p. 77.

[13]Kierkegaard, *Fear and Trembling*, p. 65.

Abraham's actions is "the paradox which does not permit of mediation. It is just as inexplicable how he got into it as it is inexplicable how he remained in it."[14] Faith itself is a paradox, a personal encounter with God, not a decision based on logical considerations.[15]

Kierkegaard's view of faith as a subjective "leap" cannot be reconciled with the nature of biblical faith. Kierkegaard maintains that "faith is not a form of knowledge,"[16] while Paul affirms that one may "believe and know the truth" (I Tim. 4:3). If logical evidence is no part of faith in the Judaeo-Christian God, then one may as legitimately "leap" to the gods of Buddhism or Hinduism.

Also, attacks against reason are invariably self-defeating, since they offer *reasons* why the position in question should be rejected. Kierkegaard's inconsistency in this regard is seen in his admonition "these are the logical deductions which I would beg the reader to have *in mente* at every point."[17] While faith is not merely an intellectual response to logical proof, it is unbiblical to define faith as a blind irrational leap.

[14]Kierkegaard, *Fear and Trembling*, p. 77.

[15]Did Kierkegaard mean by the word *paradox* a literal contradiction or did he use it in its usual sense—a *seeming* contradiction? Elmer H. Duncan favors the second interpretation (*Makers of the Modern Theological Mind: Soren Kierkegaard*, Hendrickson Publishers, 1976, p. 85). This view has some merit, particularly in view of: (1) the tendency of Kierkegaard to express himself with irony and overstatement for emphasis; (2) the fact that Kierkegaard was reacting against the perceived intellectual coldness of Hegelian epistemology (the predominant philosophy of the day) and the outwardly formal religion of the Danish church. However, his view of reason on the whole seems unable to escape the charge of being irrational. This conclusion is especially supported by the fact that Kierkegaard's underlying epistemological position was unquestionably skeptical. Also, Kierkegaard's statements concerning reason are often found in the context of literal description. It appears that his attempt to replace the cold formalism of the Danish church with the burning passion of personal commitment led him to adopt an extreme view of faith—subjectivism.

[16]Soren Kierkegaard, *Philosophical Fragments*, p. 76.

[17]Soren Kierkegaard, *Fear and Trembling*, p. 66.

A similar way of looking at allegedly conflicting statements in the Bible makes heavy use of the word *mystery*. R. Paul Stevens called this the "contemplative" approach, arguing that biblical teaching on the role of women in the church is intentionally ambiguous. Some passages, he asserts, appear to sanction women occupying leadership roles in the church but others appear to condemn such activities. Rejecting systematic approaches to harmonizing these passages, he explains that the contemplative approach

> ... views the ambiguity of Scripture as a pointer to God, an indicator of truths so great that they can only be seen in full from God-height. A contemplative view takes seriously the fact that the Bible is more often historical than abstract, more often narrative and metaphorical than systematic. A contemplative approach welcomes the mystery of male and female as an occasion of worship rather than of debate.[18]

The basic position of Stevens is that harmonizing Scripture in several important areas is above human comprehension: "The deepest issues of our life in Christ resist reduction to manageable ideas or stereotyped roles. Biblical teaching is often ambiguous in just these areas."[19] These seeming conflicts in Scripture are above our ability to resolve discrepancies. Support for this view is claimed from the belief that "a mystery takes us beyond normal categories to explore incomprehensible facts."[20] The writer claims that the mystery of the husband-wife relationship in Ephesians 5:22-33 is in the same category of "mystery" as the Trinity.[21] This approach, then, discourages a logical approach to resolving alleged conflicts in Scripture because of suggested limitations in both the clarity of Scripture and the capacities of the human mind.

[18]R. Paul Stevens, "Breaking the Gender Impasse," *Christianity Today* (Carol Stream, IL: Christianity Today, Incorporated, 1992), January 13, 1992, p. 28.

[19]*Ibid.*, p. 31.

[20]*Ibid.*, p. 30.

[21]*Ibid.*, p. 31.

This approach is from the outset a serious indictment of God: God purposely gives directives that are so unclear as to appear to conflict, then requires that the "proper" course of action be followed! Also, as far as biblical terminology is concerned, the word *mystery* is misused in the contemplative approach. When used in the New Testament, this word denotes an otherwise hidden meaning that has been made known by revelation. Also, the application of the contemplative approach to the issue of woman's role in the church reveals its character. The cited article did choose one side of the debate, arguing that women do have a scriptural right to engage in leadership roles in the church.[22]

Connected with this de-emphasis of human effort in resolving apparent conflicts in Scripture is the claim that such attempts involve legalism. Helmut Thielicke argues that "legalistic ethics with preformed decisions"[23] has no place in Christian ethics. Though the term "legalism" has been applied in a variety of ways, the basic idea in the use of this word is that strict conformity to law and the freewill response of love are mutually exclusive. However, the Scriptures do not divorce these two elements in regard to man's relationship to God. One of the reasons that God said of Job, "There is none like him on the earth" (Job 1:8), is that Job was a very conscientious man (Job 1:5). At the same time, Job was a man of great faith (Job 13:15; 19:25). Solomon's final admonition, "Fear God and keep His commandments, for this is the whole duty of man" (Eccles. 12:13), is a permanent principle which applies to all ages of man's history. The New Testament is a law (Gal. 6:2; I Cor. 9:21; James 1:25; Rom. 8:7); otherwise there could be no sin today (Rom. 4:15; I John 3:4). Rather than discouraging obedience to the law of God, love involves the keeping of His commandments: "If you love Me, keep My commandments" (John 14:15); "For this is the love of God, that we keep His command-

[22]R. Paul Stevens, "Breaking the Gender Impasse," pp. 30-31.
[23]Helmut Thielicke, *Theological Ethics* (Grand Rapids, MI: William B. Eerdmans Publishing Company, 1979), p. 650.

ments. And His commandments are not burdensome" (I John 5:3).

Though mere outward compliance with the commandments of God without the proper motive of love is useless (I Cor. 13:1-3), obedience is necessary to salvation (James 2:14-26). Grace is essential if man is to be saved (Eph. 2:8-9), but the Reformed theology of grace alone is as much an extreme as the theology against which it is a protest—the meritorious works-righteousness of Catholicism. Both are abuses of New Testament teaching. Catholicism emphasizes works to the neglect of grace; Protestantism emphasizes grace at the expense of obedience. The theology of grace alone implies that no human acts affect salvation. Though advocates of this view attempt to deny that its logical consequence is licentiousness,[24] they do so inconsistently. This inconsistency is also evident in Geisler's claim that salvation is by grace alone in a book on Christian ethics.[25] If the phrase "grace alone" is taken literally, why write a book about right and wrong when human actions are irrelevant to salvation?

Common Sense

Another approach to arriving at harmony between biblical passages is the appeal to "common sense." When biblical principles appear to collide, decisions are reached on the grounds that "it's just common sense." This claim is especially common in cases in which the solution is obvious. But is common sense an adequate standard for resolving questions of biblical harmony?

The main problem involved with this approach is the definition of the terms employed. What is meant by "common sense"? In popular usage, this phrase refers to good practical judgment or to opinions arrived at through uncomplicated means. Generally, common sense means knowledge that is shared in com-

[24]Thielicke, *Theological Ethics*, p. 613.

[25]Norman L. Geisler, *Christian Ethics: Options and Issues* (Grand Rapids, MI: Baker Book House, 1989), p. 90.

mon by most people about items they consider obvious. If the views about these obvious things are true, there must be an objective measurement by which they can be tested. Unless common sense refers to an objective body of knowledge, the phrase is useless in resolving Bible difficulties. What one person considers common sense may not be so plain to someone else. An appeal merely to common sense proves nothing. The particular belief that is claimed to be common sense may be true, but it is not true because of the claim itself, but because of the evidence in its behalf. Unless the phrase common sense is defined so that it can be tested, it means nothing more than mere assumption. Approaching the Bible from this standpoint becomes an excuse for relying on human opinions. This vague concept of common sense allows the interpreter to base conclusions on preconceived ideas. As a result, concern for "rightly dividing the word of truth" (II Tim. 2:15) is diminished.

If common sense, however, emphasizes that the search for complicated solutions is vain when a simple explanation is present, then the caution is needed. As John Haley said, "To the interpreter of Scripture, no two qualifications are more indispensable than common sense and honesty."[26] Though the appeal to common sense is sometimes an excuse for oversimplification, it may legitimately serve as a warning against overcomplication.

Counting Verses

Another approach in resolving biblical difficulties is the comparing of the number of verses on each side of the apparent conflict. The principle or statement that "wins out" is the one having the most verses in its favor. In an effort to establish the United Pentecostal doctrine that baptism must be performed only with the spoken formula "in the name of Jesus," the following writer uses the verse-counting comparison:

[26]John W. Haley, *Alleged Discrepancies of the Bible* (Nashville, TN: Gospel Advocate Company, 1974), p. 16.

A basic biblical principle is that truth must be established by more than one witness (II Corinthians 13:1). Matthew 28:19 is the only verse in the Bible to use the baptismal phrase "in the name of the Father, and of the Son, and of the Holy Ghost," while many verses reiterate the baptismal phrase in Acts 2:38, "in the name of Jesus Christ." Apparently, Matthew 28:19 is the more indirect passage that we should harmonize and interpret in light of the others.[27]

The citation of Paul's statement in II Corinthians 13:1 is misapplied in the above argument. The Old Testament source of the quotation indicates that the witnesses spoken of refer to human testimony, not divine declarations: "One witness shall not rise against a man concerning any iniquity or any sin that he commits; by the mouth of two or three witnesses the matter shall be established" (Deut. 19:15).

The weakness of the argument, "but the Bible only makes that statement once," is easily exposed. How many times does God have to make a statement for it to be true? In addition, what happens in case of a "tie"? Two New Testament passages record the exception in Jesus' divorce and remarriage teaching (Matt. 5:32; 19:9), while two others do not (Mark 10:11-12; Luke 16:18). The purely arbitrary method of setting passages in array against other passages and then comparing the number of verses on each side can never be a proper model of interpretation. While the frequency with which a topic is mentioned may indicate the importance of its role in the overall message of the Scriptures, the frequency or infrequency of a statement in Scripture does not make it any more or less true.

Love as the Norm: Situation Ethics

Apparent conflicts in Scripture often affect ethical decisions. One proposed system of solving such difficulties is situation ethics, a view made popular by Joseph Fletcher in a book

[27]David K. Bernard, *The New Birth* (Hazelwood, MO: Word Aflame Press, 1984), p. 171.

named after it.[28] The title of the book describes the system itself. Right and wrong, according to Fletcher, vary according to the situation. "For the situationist," he writes, "there are no rules—none at all."[29] An act is neither right nor wrong in itself; what is right in one circumstance may be wrong in another. But how is one to determine the right course of action in a given circumstance? The answer, according to Fletcher, is not to be found in absolute rules or laws. Instead, each situation is to be judged on the basis of one question: What would be the loving thing to do? "The ruling norm of Christian decision is love: nothing else."[30] Love is the only absolute in situation ethics; everything else is relative. In Fletcher's view, ethical systems containing any other absolutes are legalistic. He places Judaism, Catholicism, and Protestantism in this category. On the other hand, he felt that having one absolute (love) distinguished his system from total lawlessness (antinomianism). Fletcher thus saw situation ethics as the correctly balanced position between these two extremes.

Fletcher does not hesitate to state the specific application of his theory. Since "the situationist avoids words like 'never' and 'perfect' and 'always' and 'complete' as he avoids the plague, as he avoids 'absolutely,' "[31] he considers no act to be wrong for all people in all circumstances:

> If a lie is told unlovingly it is wrong, evil; if it is told in love it is good, right.[32]

> . . . if people do not believe it is wrong to have sex relations outside marriage, it isn't, unless they hurt themselves, their partners or others.[33]

[28]Joseph Fletcher, *Situation Ethics: The New Morality* (Philadelphia, PA: Westminster Press, 1966).
[29]*Ibid.*, p. 55.
[30]*Ibid.*, p. 69.
[31]*Ibid.*, pp. 43-44.
[32]*Ibid.*, p. 65.
[33]*Ibid.*, p. 140.

> A situationist . . . would be sure to protest that, in
> principle, even killing "innocent" people might be right.[34]

> . . . one could surely *pretend* to have no faith in God, or
> in any combination of gods, if it were necessary for loving
> cause. We could make a formal but false apostasy under
> persecution for the sake of dependents or the life of an
> illegal underground church.[35]

As these examples show, "the new morality, situation ethics, declares that anything and everything is right or wrong,
according to the situation."[36] In ethical decisions, "only the end
justifies the means; nothing else"[37] and "the only self-validat-
ing end in the Christian situation ethic is love."[38]

Like all other human systems of ethics, Fletcher's theory
cannot escape the charge of being subjective. For instance,
upon what basis does Fletcher limit the number of absolutes to
one (love)? If one absolute in ethics exists, may not others also?
The selecting of one principle as absolute while relativizing all
others is purely arbitrary. But even if one were to grant that
love is the sole absolute in ethics, the question remains as to
what love is. Unless this love is objective in meaning and clear
in application, the appeal to it as the final criterion in ethical
decisions has little practical value. Fletcher's definition of love
as "benevolence" or "goodwill"[39] is too general in view of
John's description of love as keeping the commandments of
God (I John 5:3; II John 6). Biblical love involves obeying the
commands of God, not arbitrarily deciding what is "the loving
thing to do."

Another fallacy in situation ethics is in its inconsistency in
regard to absolutism. When Fletcher claims that situationists
avoid words like *always, never,* and *absolutely,*[40] is he not

[34]Joseph Fletcher, *Situation Ethics*, p. 75.
[35]*Ibid.*, p. 72.
[36]*Ibid.*, p. 124.
[37]*Ibid.*, p. 120.
[38]*Ibid.*, p. 131.
[39]*Ibid.*, p. 105.
[40]*Ibid.*, p. 26.

saying that they always do so? Is this not an absolute claim? Fletcher contradicts this claim by saying, "The situationist never says . . ."[41] In fact, the basic tenor of Fletcher's entire system is absolute; the book *Situation Ethics* argues in an absolute sense against absolutism.

In situation ethics, love is the sole absolute, qualifying every other moral duty while standing unqualified itself. Situation ethics, then, makes use of the principle of qualification. But how does the principle of qualification in this context differ from biblical qualification? Is the difference merely one of degree? The key difference between the two systems is the basis by which the qualification is determined. In situation ethics, the qualification is determined by a loosely defined concept of love. This vague concept of love allows qualifications of moral duties when there is no biblical authorization for such qualifications. In other words, love is not the sole unqualified absolute in biblical ethics. In Christian ethics, qualifications are determined by biblical teaching. The only legitimate qualifications of moral duties in Christian ethics are those which God authorizes. Though both situation ethics and biblical ethics make use of the principle of qualification, its application within the two systems is vastly different. In short, situation ethics abuses a principle that is in the context of biblical ethics legitimate.

The Question of Moral Dilemmas

A major issue in ethical theory is the area of "moral dilemmas" or "conflicting moral duties." A classic example of such situations is whether lying is justified when human lives are at stake. For instance, an attacker threatens the life of a family member, claiming to spare his life only if he reveals where the other family members are hiding. The questioned member knows that the attacker will kill the other members of his family. On the one hand, he realizes that lying is wrong (Col. 3:9). On the other hand, he has a duty to protect his family

---

[41]Joseph Fletcher, *Situation Ethics*, p. 26.

members, to perform the merciful act of saving life (Mark 3:4).
If he tells the attacker that the other members of the family are
hiding in a place where they are not, he breaks the commandment against lying. If he tells the attacker where they are, they
will be killed. To further complicate the matter, if he remains
silent, he will lose his own life. This situation is often called a
moral dilemma, with "dilemma" being defined in one of two
ways. It may refer to a perplexing situation, without reference
as to whether a logical solution to the problem actually exists.
It is also used to refer to a situation in which two moral duties
come into real, not merely apparent, conflict. This phase of the
study is concerned with the second of these usages.

In *Christian Ethics,* Norman Geisler evaluates six approaches
to the problem of moral dilemmas:[42]

1. *Antinomianism*—the rejection of all moral laws.

2. *Generalism*—views such as utilitarianism, which assert
   only general principles of ethics.

3. *Situation ethics*—as advocated by Joseph Fletcher.

4. *Unqualified absolutism*—views that admit no qualifications of moral commands; Geisler cites Augustine as an
   example of an unqualified absolutist who would argue
   that the threatened family member, in the case described
   above, would be morally bound to reveal where the other
   family members were hiding.

5. *Conflicting absolutism*—the "lesser of two evils" view.

6. *Graded absolutism*—the view that higher moral duties
   override lower ones.

Underlying Geisler's assessment of these views is his belief
that conflicting moral duties actually occur: "It is both unreal-
istic and unbiblical to assume that moral obligations never
conflict."[43] This position is similar to the reasoning of those

[42]Norman L. Geisler, *Christian Ethics: Options and Issues* (Grand Rapids, MI: Baker Book House, 1989), pp. 1-132.
[43]*Ibid.,* p. 94.

who claim that the Bible contradicts itself. Because they cannot find a solution to alleged discrepancies in the Bible, some conclude that contradictions actually exist in the Scriptures. Because Geisler can, to his satisfaction, find no solution to apparent moral conflicts, he concludes that real moral dilemmas exist. Though his book offers valuable insights on the views listed above, his evaluation of them is colored by this assumption.

To affirm that conflicting moral duties actually occur (so that one *must* break a moral command regardless of what choice is made) is to become entangled in a web of inconsistency. In his analysis of the higher/lower law approach, Geisler argues that "the conflict is real because neither law 'backed down'; both continued to be binding though one was more binding than the other."[44] When, however, a law is binding, failure to obey that law is a violation of it. One can break a law only if he is amenable to it; he cannot break a law that is not binding on him. Geisler claims that in conflicting situations "the lower command is not really broken when the higher command is followed."[45]

This reasoning is an attempt to evade an obvious contradiction: a "binding" law is "not really broken" when it is disobeyed. Geisler offers the analogy of a magnet that "does not break the law of gravity in attracting a nail"[46] as justification for his position. However, this example from nature is a case of qualification; the law of gravity is qualified by the attraction of the magnet. It is incorrect and misleading to claim that one of the laws of the allegedly conflicting situation remains applicable but is not broken when a higher command is followed. In bare form, this reasoning states that a law is both binding and not binding at the same time! This absurdity could be avoided by simply recognizing the nature of the principle of qualification.

---

[44]Norman L. Geisler, *Christian Ethics*, p. 128.
[45]*Ibid.*, p. 128.
[46]*Ibid.*, p. 129.

Another approach to moral dilemmas is one which Geisler himself rejects: "the lesser of two evils" view. This view asserts that moral dilemmas actually occur. The difference between Geisler's position and this view is that while Geisler does not hold that the failure to observe one of the commands is sinful, the lesser of two evils view does. The recommended course of action in this approach is to choose the lesser evil in the dilemma and then to appeal to the mercy of God. Applied to the case of lying to save human life, this view argues that lying is evil in this situation but failing to save human life is a greater evil. Helmut Thielicke describes this action as "compromise."[47] Arguing that such conflicts are "basically insoluble,"[48] Theilicke maintains that ethical compromise is an inevitable consequence of a fallen world and an important element in justification.[49] By encountering situations in which evil is inevitable in spite of which alternative is chosen, man is compelled to seek forgiveness from God. Thielicke sees this as a preventive measure to false security arising from man's solving of the dilemma by himself.[50]

Had Thielicke replaced the word *compromise* with the concept of qualification, he would not have advocated the "lesser of two evils" view. One factor in particular affected not only his choice of words but also his entire ethical theory: the basic assumptions of Calvinism, especially an unqualified view of the sovereignty of God and the doctrine of hereditary depravity. Though an extensive treatment of neither of these assumptions is presented in this study, the first has been briefly dealt with earlier and the second will be challenged shortly. Mention is made of them here to identify the source of Thielicke's basic view. For instance, it is not strange that Thielicke believed that some situations make sin theoretically unavoidable given his view of man as having been born into the world a sinner.

[47]Helmut Thielicke, *Theological Ethics: Foundations* (Grand Rapids, MI: William B. Eerdmans Publishing Company, 1966), pp. 455-667.
[48]*Ibid.*, p. 493.
[49]*Ibid.*, pp. 650-660.
[50]*Ibid.*, pp. 612-613.

"The lesser of two evils" view is sometimes applied less radically and from different basic assumptions. In regard to unscriptural divorce and remarriage, Jack P. Lewis contends that

> the issue becomes more complicated when the desire to repent is characterized by only one party in the marriage. It is further complicated when children are born to the union. Some problems of life do not offer a choice between good and evil. They only offer a choice between two evils, and it is difficult to know which is the greater. In the adulterous marriage problem, the one evil is continuing in a relationship that should never have been started and about which (if the definition of adultery as on-going is valid) the consequences are dire indeed. The other is the abandonment of obligations to children who did not ask to be born under such conditions.[51]

Only a naive or calloused observer would argue that the solution to such situations is easy. The complexity and the feelings involved in such decisions cannot be denied. The question of unscriptural marriages will be examined later. At this point, attention is directed to Lewis's assessment of the situation as a choice of the lesser of two evils.

The chief problem with the lesser evil view is that it denies Paul's assurance to the Corinthians that

> no temptation has overtaken you except such as is common to man; but God is faithful, who will not allow you to be tempted beyond what you are able, but with the temptation will also make the way of escape, that you may be able to bear it (I Cor. 10:13).

To suggest that God places man in a situation in which he is bound by conflicting commands that cannot both be obeyed is to bring into question God's justice as affirmed in this verse. God does not hold man responsible for what he cannot do.

The Bible does indicate that some sins are more serious both

[51]Jack P. Lewis, "Adultery and Repentance," *Gospel Advocate* (Nashville, TN: Gospel Advocate Company, 1992), January, 1992, p. 22.

in nature and in consequences. Jesus spoke of "the greater sin" of His betrayal (John 19:11). He also spoke of degrees of punishment in hell (Luke 12:47-48; Matt. 11:20-24). But this information is given to help man understand the nature of sin, not to establish a standard for making ethical decisions. Though the more serious sin can sometimes be determined in a comparison of actions, it is not always possible to do so. The Bible does not give a complete list of sins in order of their severity. Consequently, the selection of the lesser of two evils will eventually be arbitrary, since no exhaustive, objective standard for identifying every "lesser" sin is available.

Guidance of the Holy Spirit

Another approach to harmonizing seemingly conflicting verses is the suggestion that the Holy Spirit, working outside the realm of the written Word, imparts special knowledge to the interpreter in such cases. "According to Matt. 10:19-20," Thielicke claims, complicated ethical decisions "will through the help of the Spirit be resolved at the decisive moment by a clear simplification, i.e., by the manifestation of the single unequivocal choice with which we are confronted."[52] In the passage cited by Thielicke, Jesus promised:

> But when they deliver you up, do not worry about how or what you should speak. For it will be given to you in that hour what you should speak; for it is not you who speak, but the Spirit of your Father who speaks in you (Matt. 10:19-20).

This promise occurs in the context of the limited commission of the twelve. It was given to the apostles, not to all Christians. The promise is one of miraculous impartation of the divine will to human beings by the Spirit. This oral revelation was an essential element in God's plan until the early church reached a point of maturity and the written revelation was complete (I Cor. 13:8-13). When this stage of completion was reached,

[52]Helmut Thielicke, *Theological Ethics*, p. 651.

"that which is in part"—the miraculous gifts of the Spirit spoken of in the context—would be "done away."[53] Thielicke's appeal to Jesus' promise for assistance in ethical decisions today is a misapplication of the verse.

The view that the Holy Spirit aids the believing interpreter, known as *illumination,* is common in books on biblical interpretation. This doctrine has a twofold application. First, it asserts that for a sinner to understand Scripture, the Holy Spirit must illuminate his understanding. Second, it holds that the Spirit provides continued assistance in the believer's interpretation of Scripture. In both stages, the alleged assistance amounts to understanding imparted through means in addition to the written word. One writer argues that "the deepest factor influencing biblical interpretation is the work of the Holy Spirit in regeneration."[54] Mickelsen emphasizes "a quiet dependence upon the Holy Spirit or Helper to illuminate the believer's understanding."[55] William Larkin extends this doctrine even to determining the application of Scripture: "The Spirit's illumination also guides the believer in applying Scripture."[56] An examination of this popular assumption, however, should focus on the theologian with whom it originated: John Calvin.

[53]For a discussion of this passage in regard to the temporary nature of miraculous activity in the early church, see Guy N. Woods, *The Woods-Franklin Debate* (Birmingham, AL: Roberts & Son, 1975); Rubel Shelly, "What is the 'Perfect' Thing of First Corinthians 13:10?" in *What Do You Know About the Holy Spirit?,* Wendell Winkler, ed. (Hurst, TX: Winkler Publications, 1980), pp. 226-234; Roy Deaver, "That Which is Perfect," *Spiritual Sword,* Thomas B. Warren, ed. (Memphis, TN: Getwell church of Christ, 1974), April 1974, pp. 35-36; Gary W. Workman, "When That Which is Perfect is Come" in *Studies in I Corinthians,* Dub McClish, ed. (Denton TX: Valid Publications, 1982), pp. 170-181.

[54]Vern S. Poythress, *Science and Hermeneutics* (Grand Rapids, MI: Academie Books, Zondervan Publishing House, 1988), p. 101.

[55]A. Berkeley Mickelsen, *Interpreting the Bible* (Grand Rapids, MI: William B. Eerdmans Publishing Company, 1963) p. 361.

[56]William L. Larkin, Jr., *Culture and Biblical Hermeneutics* (Grand Rapids, MI: Baker Book House, 1988), p. 289.

Calvin's seemingly favorite verse in his attempt to establish the doctrine of illumination is Paul's reference to the "natural man":

> But the natural man does not receive the things of the Spirit of God, for they are foolishness to him; nor can he know them, because they are spiritually discerned (I Cor. 2:14).

Calvin defines the "natural man" as "the man who trusts to the light of nature. Such a man has no understanding in the spiritual mysteries of God."[57] To Calvin, illumination is the means by which the Holy Spirit opens the spiritual eyes of the sinner. This interpretation, though popular since Calvin's time, is inconsistent with the context of Paul's statement. In the opening section of I Corinthians (chaps. 1-3), Paul contrasts human wisdom with the divine wisdom revealed in the gospel. Indicated repeatedly in this section is the fact that those who rely on worldly thinking have a disdain for the wisdom that comes from above (1:18, 21-25; 2:1, 5). The key theme in this section is the attitude of such people toward divine revelation. The "spirit of the world" (I Cor. 2:12) is this prideful, worldly disposition. Since this spirit is in contrast to "the spirit which is of God" (KJV) in the same verse, the New King James Version rendering "the Spirit who is from God" is incorrect. The "natural man" rejects revelation from God and regards it as foolishness. This description could not be true of one who has never heard the revelation. He cannot know them because his attitude, not his state, prevents him from understanding the revelation as he ought (cf. John 8:43). Also, the contrast with the verse that follows (". . . the natural man . . . but he that is spiritual . . .") indicates that Paul is speaking of a worldly, carnal disposition. Additionally, as the context shows, this unspiritual attitude was precisely the problem at Corinth (I Cor. 3:1-4, where "carnal" is synonymous with "natural" in 2:14).

[57]John Calvin, *Institutes of the Christian Religion*, Henry Beveridge, trans. (Grand Rapids, MI: William B. Eerdmans Publishing Company, 1983 reprint), Vol. I, p. 240.

The source of the doctrine of illumination, however, is not Calvin's misinterpretation of I Corinthians 2:14 or other passages, but his basic assumption regarding the nature of man as being essentially bad. The "sinful nature" which he supposed men to possess prevents them from understanding the Scriptures. A chief reason for the widespread adoption of Calvinistic views is the failure to understand the theological context in which these views were developed. The doctrine of illumination was one of several positions Calvin took in an effort to be consistent with his overriding concern: the refutation of Catholic works-righteousness. But this concern crossed the line of biblical boundaries into a theology as extreme as the Catholic system, a view of man's role in justification as consistently radical as it is prevalent. Calvin's *Institutes* is replete with fervent criticisms of Catholicism, with many of these objections being legitimate. The result of his unchecked zeal, however, was a theology at variance with fundamental Bible themes, particularly free will (Josh. 24:15; Deut. 30:15-20), the nature of sin as being an act of the will, not an inherited trait (I John 3:4; Ezek. 18:20), personal accountability (Romans 14:12; Matt. 25:14-30), and the justice of God (Rom. 2:6-11; Rev. 20:12-15).

Proof-Texting

This phrase typically refers to citing a passage in supposed proof of a point that is at variance with the overall trend of Scripture. The cited passage appears to support the view because the citation has been disconnected from the broader context of the Bible as a whole. Proof-texting differs from "taking a verse out of context" only in the amount of textual material being considered. When a verse is said to have been "taken out of context," the material in question is the immediate context surrounding the verse itself. Proof-texting occurs when a verse is lifted out of the entire context of the Bible. This selective model of Bible interpretation sets the cited passage in contradiction to other Bible teaching by ignoring relevant verses.

Giving special attention to an individual passage or citing a passage as evidence for a conclusion is not in itself proof-texting. Jesus Himself regularly cited Old Testament verses in proof of His statements, as is seen in His frequent question to the Jews, "Have you not read" (Matt. 12:3; 19:4; 22:31)? Peter's sermon on Pentecost contains citations from Joel (Acts 2:16-21) and David (Acts 2:25-28, 34-35). If a passage establishes a given truth, citing the passage as proof of this point is appropriate unless the text is made a "hobby" and other biblical principles are neglected. Also, criticism of balanced "book, chapter, and verse" preaching encounters another difficulty. How can the "overall theme" of the Bible be discovered without studying its individual parts? Bernard Ramm referred to this important process in interpretation as the "hermeneutical spiral":

> "We can understand a particular passage only if we know what the whole Scripture teaches; but, we can only know what the whole Scripture teaches by knowing the meaning of its parts." And so all theological interpretation of Scripture is a rotation or "spiraling" from part to whole, and whole to part.[58]

While consideration of the overall context of Scripture is essential to proper interpretation, analysis of its individual parts is also necessary, provided that this analysis is balanced by and consistent with Bible teaching as a whole.

The Danger of Personal Bias

Most of the approaches examined to this point attempt to present a logical case for their soundness. But not all approaches to solving apparent conflicts in the Bible proceed on this basis. In fact, some "solutions" to such problems are based on no method at all. The passage that "wins out" is the one preferred by the interpreter. The determination as to which verse is qualified and which is the qualifier is arbitrary and subjective, having no logical grounds for the conclusion drawn.

[58]Bernard Ramm, *Protestant Biblical Interpretation: A Textbook of Hermeneutics* (Grand Rapids, MI: Baker Book House, 1970), p. 139.

This biased approach to Bible interpretation results from several factors in the psychological state of the interpreter. One of these is the type of biblical material favored by a given personality type. Cedric B. Johnson observes that interest shown to favorite areas of everyday life is "selective attention" that the interpreter also transfers to the Bible.[59] Some Bible students prefer literal sections of the Bible, while others favor the symbolic. Some are stimulated by the emotional content of the Psalms, while others are more challenged by the logical progression of thought in Paul's epistles. Perhaps every Bible student has "favorite" verses. When these personal preferences are undisciplined, however, the less-favored parts of the Bible and the duties they enjoin are ignored.

Another danger in Bible interpretation is the presence of erroneous preconceptions in the interpreter. Looking at the Bible through "colored glasses" is a subtle cause of misinterpretation. Though the role of preunderstanding in interpretation has been exaggerated in recent years, the influence of preconceived ideas must regularly be checked by the self-examination of the interpreter. Perhaps even less detected by the interpreter is the fallacy of overreaction in interpretation. The abuse of biblical teaching is often countered by an extreme reaction, with the zealous interpreter being partially blinded to the biblical message by his concern for correcting this abuse. This overriding concern creates an unbalanced approach to Scripture. The partial interpreter "sees" his pet subject in verses that do not address it and allows no qualification of passages that appear to establish his view.

Interpretation is not merely an intellectual endeavor. The emotions and the will of the interpreter affect the conclusions he reaches. This is why the Bible places such great emphasis on the heart of one who approaches its pages. An "honest and good heart" (Luke 8:15) is indispensable in correctly interpreting the Scriptures.

[59]Cedric B. Johnson, *The Psychology of Biblical Interpretation* (Grand Rapids, MI: William B. Eerdmans Publishing Company, 1983), pp. 41-66.

PART
TWO

BIBLICAL
PRECEDENTS

4

Qualification
and the Covenants

Few areas of Bible study involve as many critical sub-issues as the relationship between the covenants, particularly the transition from the law to the gospel. The similarities and differences between them present special problems in the synthesis of Bible information on a topic appearing in both sections. These difficulties deserve focused attention regarding the principle of qualification. Aside from these considerations, however, a study of the covenants makes an important contribution in the examination of this principle. An analysis of certain relevant aspects of the doctrine of the covenants reveals important guidelines for modern times.

Covenant Amenability

The law of Moses was limited in binding force in two key respects. It was a covenant made with Israel (Deut. 5:1-2), not a universal law code for all nations. Although the Gentiles could become proselytes (Acts 2:11), they were under no obligation to convert to Judaism. Apart from periodic direct revelations (Jonah, Daniel, etc.), the law to which the Gentiles were subject consisted mainly of the moral principles discernible from nature (Rom. 2:14-15). In terms of the people to whom it applied, the law was limited to Israel.

The law was also restricted by time. Using the illustration of a *paidagogos* (Gal. 3:24-25), "a temporary custodian or guardian," Paul informs his readers that the law was "abolished" (Eph. 2:15), "nailed" to the cross (Col. 2:14), and "taken away" (II Cor. 3:14). Circumcision, Sabbath observance, and the other specific religious requirements of the law have been annulled. They are not mandatory for any person living today.

These facts shed light on a fundamental question concerning amenability to divine law: Since the New Testament was originally delivered to people living in the first century, how can we be sure that it is binding today? At the most explicit level, this question is answered in the New Testament description of the gospel as a law for all generations subsequent to its beginning. The new law is an "everlasting covenant" (Heb. 13:20; cf. Rev. 14:6) and will be the standard of judgment for all those living in the Christian dispensation (John 12:48; Rom. 2:16). The requirements stated in the Great Commission (Matt. 28:18-20) apply to "all the nations" until "the end of the age."

This question also finds an important parallel in the binding force of the law. The commonly used phrase, "throughout your generations" (Exod. 12:14; 30:8; Lev. 10:9, etc.), includes Israelites living after the time of Moses. The passing of time did not by itself remove the Israelites' responsibility to keep the law. The Sabbath law given hundreds of years earlier at Sinai was enforced in Nehemiah's time (Neh. 13); the prohibition regarding mixed marriages (Deut. 7:1-4) was enforced with severe measures in Ezra's time (Ezra 10).

Though He lived fifteen centuries after Moses, Jesus repeatedly emphasized the abiding authoritativeness of the law in His earthly ministry. Once a covenant has been put into force by divine decree, it can cease in its binding force only by the same process. The absence of a divine revocation of the New Testament, in addition to its universal and perpetual status as a law, establishes its authoritativeness in all generations subsequent to its delivery. God is under no obligation to "renew His contract" with man. Since the New Testament is perpetually authoritative, no need exists for the Koran, the Book of Mormon, or the decrees of the papacy.

The universal applicability of the gospel, in distinction from the law of Moses as a national covenant made with Israel, has significant implications for modern times. The frequently asked and controversial question, "Will those who have never heard the gospel be lost?" may be answered by appealing to the difference between the law of Moses and the gospel as it concerns the people amenable to these covenants. The law was expressly restricted to Israel, while the gospel is authoritative for "all men everywhere" (Acts 17:30). Once the transitional phase between Old Testament and New Testament was complete, the only divine law left in force was the gospel. Since the completion of this transition, all accountable people have been amenable to the gospel. As a result, those who die outside of Christ have no hope. "I am the way, the truth, and the life," explained Jesus. "No one comes to the Father except through me" (John 14:6). To argue otherwise is to reject the need for fulfilling the Great Commission. If the heathen are safe in their ignorance, then it is better not to preach the gospel to them, since some would reject the gospel and be condemned (Mark 16:15-16). Men are "without excuse" (Rom. 1:20) because they can know of God's existence through nature (Ps. 19:1; Acts 14:15-17; Rom. 1:18-20) and may by His providential assistance find Him (Acts 17:27; Matt. 7:7-8; John 7:17).

The absence of any qualification of the gospel regarding the people to whom it applies also sheds light on another controversial topic. Two major theories have been proposed in an attempt to prove that those outside Christ are not subject to New Testament legislation on divorce and remarriage. In 1954, E. C. Fuqua argued that those in the world are amenable to civil law only and are not under the New Testament in any sense.[1] Relative to Jesus' teaching on divorce and remarriage, Fuqua asserted that those who have divorced and remarried

[1] *The Warren-Fuqua Debate: Are Non-Christians Amenable to the Law of Christ?* (Jonesboro, AR: National Christian Press).

for unscriptural reasons before becoming Christians were not guilty of violating this teaching because they were under civil law only when the remarriage occurred. Fuqua's theory carries the absurd implication that it is impossible for a person in the world to become a sinner, since sin is the violation of divine law (I John 3:4) and one can only break a law to which he is amenable (Rom. 4:15).

Realizing the disastrous implications of Fuqua's position, James D. Bales modified the Fuqua theory by asserting the continuance of the moral law system to which the Gentiles were accountable while the Israelites were under the law of Moses.[2] In this view, those in the world are amenable to the law described in Romans 2:14-15 and Christians are the only people subject to the law of Christ. Bales argues that those in the world who divorce and remarry contrary to Jesus' teaching are not guilty of violating the law of Christ because they are not under that law. This attempt to circumvent the stringency of New Testament teaching on divorce and remarriage also has destructive implications. If those in the world are not amenable to the gospel, then they are under no obligation to obey it. Since one can only obey or violate a law to which he is amenable, Bales' view implies that no one today is obligated to become a Christian.[3]

Circumstantial Qualification

One of the abiding principles established in the Old Testament is that inability arising out of physical circumstances qualifies religious duties. God deals with man according to his situation, and He does not require of man what he is physically unable to do. Responsibility to a divine command presupposes the ability to perform the prescribed action. When this ability is absent, the corresponding duty is not binding. This principle,

[2]James D. Bales, *Not Under Bondage* (Searcy, AR: James D. Bales, 1979) and *The Scope of the Covenants* (Searcy, AR: James D. Bales, 1982).

[3]Thomas B. Warren, *Keeping the Lock in Wedlock* (Jonesboro, AR: National Christian Press, 1980), p. 152.

however, is not situation ethics. Even less is it a license to arbitrarily select circumstances as an excuse for not meeting a biblical duty. The qualification arises out of the limits of physical possibility, not the desirability or difficulty of obeying a command in the face of circumstantial hindrances.

Under the law, the duty of offerings was qualified by the circumstance of poverty. This provision was explicitly and repeatedly stated in the law. An Israelite who had sinned was to bring "a lamb or a kid of the goats as a sin offering" (Lev. 5:6). This requirement, however, is immediately qualified: "If he is not able to bring a lamb, then he shall bring to the Lord, for his trespass which he has committed, two turtledoves or two young pigeons" (v. 7). The same substitution was allowed in offerings of purification (Lev. 12:8) and in offerings connected with the cleansing of lepers (Lev. 14:30-32). "Every man shall give as he is able" (Deut. 16:17) was the regulating principle of the relative worth of offerings under the law. This stipulation is shown to be a permanent principle by Paul's command that each Christian is to give "as he may prosper" (I Cor. 16:2).

The Babylonian captivity is a unique case of limitations imposed by circumstances. Separated from their homeland for seventy years, the Jews were physically unable to engage in required temple services. As a result, an institution evidently arose in this period that became a permanent part of Judaism before and since the time of Christ: the synagogue. Though having no explicit authorization in the law, the synagogue was authorized within the realm of expedience. Jesus' approval of this arrangement is shown by His participation in and use of the synagogue. In their use of the synagogue, the Jews during the captivity worshipped as circumstances permitted. They were kept back by force from travelling to Jerusalem.

The duty to inflict the death penalty in the law underwent change as Israel moved from an internally governed theocracy to foreign domination. Though this punishment had been both authorized and practiced in Moses' time, Israel's subjection to Rome had severely restricted their political right to exercise coercion. At Jesus' trial, the Jews complained to Pilate: "It is not lawful for us to put anyone to death" (John 18:31). But these words of envious and hypocritical religious leaders do not accurately represent the full picture. In a speech recorded by Josephus, the later Roman general Titus said that the Jews had been delegated the authority to put to death foreigners who went beyond the wall of partition at the temple.[4] The mentioning of temple guards (Acts 5:22-26) and the inflicting of punishments in the synagogues (Acts 26:11) indicates that some degree of civil force was exercised. But the Jews may have often gone beyond what was permitted by Roman authorities. As a result, the mob execution of Stephen (Acts 7) carries little weight in establishing a general right of the Jews to inflict capital punishment. It is not necessary for present purposes to determine the precise extent of the Jews' authority from Rome to exercise coercion in Jesus' day. The point to be observed is that the Jews of this time did not stand in the same relation to commands in the law regarding capital punishment as the Israelites of Moses' day did, and this because of circumstances beyond their choice.

These examples in the law provide an important principle in the study of biblical ethics. Applied to modern times, this principle means that parallel circumstances constitute a similar qualification of New Testament commands. Poverty, illness, and imprisonment are circumstances that qualify the respective duties of giving, ministering to others, and assembling with the saints for worship (II Cor. 9:7; Gal. 6:10; Heb. 10:25). It is incorrect to say that these commands may be broken because of extenuating circumstances. These requirements do not apply to the situations mentioned; their realm of application does not include such circumstances. The principle is one of qualifying, not merely extenuating or mitigating circumstances. Still less is it proper to say that those caught in such conditions have been "providentially hindered" (as if God in

---

[4]Flavius Josephus, *Wars*, VI, 2.4, *The Works of Josephus*, William Whitson, trans. (Lynn, MA: Hendrickson Publishers, 1980), p. 575.

His providence hinders man from obeying His will). In spite of such misnomers, the principle of circumstantial qualification is a fundamental criterion for many current moral issues.

Moral Principles

An important point of similarity between the Old Testament and the New Testament is the moral principles found in each. The vices of lying and homosexuality have always been wrong; the virtues of mercy and justice have always been right. The consistency of Bible teaching on these matters shows their permanent status as absolute moral principles. This unity of doctrine also points to a common ground of absoluteness: the nature of God Himself. God does not arbitrarily decide that some moral matters are right and others are wrong, as if He might have made murder a holy act and giving to the poor an unrighteous deed. On the other hand, He is not compelled by external forces to accept some acts as lawful and others as unlawful, as if He must bow down in subjection to a moral standard higher than Himself. The basis for moral principles is the character of God. His inherent goodness determines whether such acts are right or wrong. Since the nature of God does not change (Mal. 3:6; James 1:17), the status of moral principles remains the same in every Bible age. In obeying these principles man acts in harmony with the nature of God; in rejecting them he behaves contrary to it.

The changes in divine requirements during Bible history establish an important distinction in biblical commands. Many of the rites and observances of the Mosaic law, for instance, have been repealed by the law of Christ. Such requirements are called *positive* commands and differ from the "moral" precepts of Scripture.

But how do these types of commands differ? An illustration of this distinction is much easier to provide than an explanation. Laws in the Ten Commandments against lying, stealing, murder, and adultery are usually distinguished from the Sabbath law in terms of moral/positive commands or moral/religious commands. The distinction appears to involve several factors.

First, the manner in which the two types of commands are comprehended is different. Positive laws may be recognized only through direct revelation from God either in oral or in written form. However, moral law incorporates information discernible from natural revelation. The Gentiles were thus able to observe "by nature" the moral principles conveyed by the direct revelation of the law (Rom. 2:14-15); they recognized that some acts were "against nature" (Rom. 1:26).

Second, the two differ as to the beings toward which the respective required actions are directed. Positive commands uniquely emphasize the participant's attitude toward God. God's order to Moses to pick up the serpent (Exod. 4:4) was obeyed from the mere fact that God commanded it. While such commands sometimes involve actions toward other persons, their point of emphasis is obedience in view of man's relationship to God. Moral commands, however, while arising out of man's responsibility to the Creator, focus on his relationship to other human beings. Man lies to his *fellow man*, steals from his *neighbor*, murders a *human being*, and commits adultery with a *person* to whom he is not married.

Third, moral commands and positive commands differ in the purposes they serve in God's plan. Moral commands are given to test man's love, while positive commands are given to test man's faith. However, these are differences of emphasis in the nature of these two types of commands, not exclusive distinctions as to what they involve.

Even more important is the relationship of moral law and positive law when both are involved in the same divine requirement. The trial of Abraham at Moriah is one of the most perplexing cases of this combination in Bible history. That Abraham understood murder to be wrong cannot be doubted in view of the guilt incurred by Cain (Gen. 4) and the institution of the death penalty for this crime (Gen. 9:6). Yet God commanded him to offer Isaac as a burnt offering (Gen. 22:2). How can this directive be reconciled with the absolute prohibition against murder?

Kierkegaard's approach was that the case of Abraham is the foremost example of the true nature of faith as a paradox, a contradiction that cannot be logically harmonized but should rather be accepted by a "leap of faith."

Another proposal is that the trial of Abraham constitutes an actual case of conflicting moral duties.[5]

A more attractive suggestion is that the prohibition against murder was suspended in Abraham's trial as the laws of nature were suspended during the performance of miracles. This approach involves a serious difficulty. If the prohibition against murder may be temporarily lifted, then why could not laws against lying and homosexuality be suspended, making these acts temporarily lawful?

Another approach to this episode in Abraham's life centers on the fact that Abraham never actually carried out the command to take his son's life. In this reasoning, the command to Abraham is similar to Solomon's decree to "divide the living child in two" (I Kings 3:25). But if what Abraham was told to do was actually murder, then he accepted this unlawful act in his mind, where sin begins (Matt. 5:21-28; I John 3:15). That Abraham planned to kill Isaac is clear from the context and from other verses (Gen. 22:5; Heb. 11:17-19).

The key to solving this alleged moral dilemma is recognizing the qualifying force of positive law in defining the application of moral principles. The taking of human life is not in all cases unlawful, as the Mosaic practice of capital punishment demonstrates. Murder is the unjust killing of an innocent human being out of malicious intent. No such motives were present in Abraham. The problem remains as to how God could demand human sacrifice, especially in view of later condemnations of the heathen custom of child sacrifice (Lev. 20:1-5; Jer. 7:31; 32:35).

---

[5]See Chapter 3 for an examination of these first two approaches.

The appeal to positive law as justification for this command involves two important factors. One is the sovereign right of God to give and to take life (Gen. 50:19). God has at times required the life of innocent people in connection with the fulfilling of His will for man. For instance, infants died in the flood because of direct intervention of God. If God may, for reasons consistent with His infinite goodness and wisdom, justly take the life of an innocent human being by direct intervention, why may He not issue a command to this end involving the agency of His servants? Israelite wars with the Canaanites involved the killing of innocent children, and this killing was performed by divine authority (Deut. 3:6; I Sam. 15:3). If positive law qualified the prohibition against taking human life in the case of these children, could it not also be the basis for the command to Abraham in Genesis 22?

The other consideration is the typology contained in the account of Abraham and Isaac. Abraham was told to do the very thing that God actually did with His Son (John 3:16; I John 4:10). If the antitype is morally right, how can the commanded type be ethically wrong? This ultimate sacrifice is the basis for John's insistence that "we also ought to lay down our lives for the brethren" (I John 3:16).

The issues of polygamy and divorce are also unique cases of the relationship between moral law and positive law and of the distinction between the covenants. Involving the marriage relationship and its attendant sexual activity, these issues obviously involve moral principles. Yet both of these practices undergo change from the Old Testament to the New Testament. Polygamy was commonly practiced prior to and during the Mosaic economy (Gen. 25:6; I Sam. 25:43), but the New Testament requires monogamy (I Cor. 7:2; Eph. 5:33). Divorce for reasons other than fornication was permitted under the law (Deut. 24:1-4; Matt. 19:8), but Jesus restored the Edenic ideal of marriage, giving but one cause for divorce (Matt. 19:9). Nineteenth century orator and agnostic Robert Ingersoll cited these changes in divine allowance in his attacks against the Scriptures.[6]

A commonly proposed solution to these problems is that polygamy and divorce were tolerated in a civil sense only in the Old Testament, with the implication being that God regarded these customs as sinful.[7] This case appeals to Jesus' explanation that "Moses, because of the hardness of your hearts, permitted you to divorce your wives, but from the beginning it was not so" (Matt. 19:8). Moses then, according to this view, merely regulated an existing practice without giving sanction to it. This position also leans heavily on Paul's contrast that "these times of ignorance God overlooked, but now commands all men everywhere to repent" (Acts 17:30). The absence of clearer light from the New Testament revelation is seen to lessen or remove the guilt of Old Testament characters who engaged in these practices.

A detailed examination of this position is too lengthy to pursue here.[8] The basic problem with this view, however, is that it dismisses important evidence for the position that both polygamy and divorce were permitted with divine authorization. Abraham had concubines at a late stage in his life (Gen. 25:6), but he is said to have "died in faith" (Heb. 11:13). Jacob (Gen. 29-30) and David (I Sam. 25:43) had more than one wife while having an important relationship with God. The practice is mentioned in Deuteronomy 21:15 in regard to inheritance

[6]Roger E. Greeley, ed., *The Best of Robert Ingersoll* (Buffalo, N.Y.: Prometheus Books, 1983), pp. 73, 108.

[7]John Murray, *Principles of Conduct: Aspects of Biblical Ethics* (Grand Rapids, MI: William B. Eerdmans Publishing Company, 1957), pp. 14-17; Gary L. Headrick, "Moses on Divorce and Remarriage," *Marriage, Divorce and Remarriage*, Maurice W. Lusk, III (Atlanta, GA: Guild of Scribes, 1982), p. 29; Norman L. Geisler, *Christian Ethics: Issues and Options* (Grand Rapids, MI: Baker Book House, 1989), pp. 280-281; M.C. Kurfees, Ed., *Questions and Answers by Lipscomb and Sewell* (Nashville, TN: Gospel Advocate Company, 1921), pp. 474-475.

[8]For a critique of this view as applied to divorce, see my book *The Remarriage of a Divorced Couple* (Tompkinsville, KY: Kerry Duke, 1989), pp. 18-22.

laws. The general tenor of Old Testament discussion of the subject combined with the absence of divine disapproval strengthens the examples above.

As to Mosaic legislation on divorce (Deut. 24:1-4), Jesus explicitly referred to this teaching as a "precept" that Moses "wrote" (Mark 10:5). This passage, according to the discussion of the context, included authorization for both the bill of divorce and the act of divorce itself upon the ground of "uncleanness" (Mark 10:3-4). To suggest that Moses gave civil permission to engage in a sinful practice is to ignore Mark's revealing account of Jesus' discussion of this subject. But if polygamy and divorce are moral issues and if moral principles do not change, how could these practices be divinely authorized in one dispensation and sinful in another?

At this point it is critical to observe that polygamy and divorce are merely aspects of an unchanging moral principle: the sanctity of marriage. This union is the only divinely authorized realm in which the sexual relationship can occur; sexual union outside this realm is sinful. This principle is permanent. But what constitutes a legitimate marriage has undergone some variation in divine teaching since Eden. Though some Old Testament marriages were composed of one man and several wives, they were marriages nonetheless. Concubines were not adulteresses but half-wives in terms of their right to be supported by their husband. That they were actually married is evident from the fact that the Levite's concubine "played the harlot against . . . her husband" (Lev. 19:2-3). Unless they were married, she could not have committed adultery against him, and he could not have been her husband. Also, David received no censure for marrying a plurality of women, but his son died because David had engaged in sexual intercourse with a woman outside the realm of marriage (II Sam. 11-12).

Whether a man can have more than one wife at a time is a matter of divine positive law. Divine regulations on divorce are also positive commands in that they determine whether a man can have different successive wives and upon what grounds he may do so. Divine positive commands establish acceptable grounds of divorce. This fact accounts for the difference between Mosaic legislation on divorce and Jesus' teaching (Matt. 19:8-9). Divorce for reasons other than fornication was permitted under the law (although the law did not sanction divorce for *any* reason). In Jesus' words, however, this "was not so from the beginning" (Matt. 19:8). God's original ideal will at Eden stressed the permanence of marriage, and for this reason Jesus immediately referred to the Genesis account in response to the Pharisees' question about divorce (Matt. 19:3-6). Because of the circumstance of the Israelites' hardness of heart, God allowed divorce. In Jesus' legislation the emphasis of the original purpose for marriage is restored with only one authorized cause for divorce and remarriage: fornication. Teaching on divorce in the law was parenthetical legislation between the Edenic ideal and Jesus' law. Though divinely authorized grounds for divorce have undergone change, the moral principle that one may engage in lawful sexual union only within the divinely authorized realm of marriage has not. Adultery was sinful under the law and is unlawful under the law of Christ, but the adultery of Matthew 19:9 is not found in the law. This modification exists on the basis of positive law in regard to marriage and divorce. Positive commands as to whether a man may have more than one wife at a time or more than one wife in succession serve to define the unchanging moral principle by establishing the boundaries of the authorized realm of activity.

The items discussed in this section offer valuable insight into the nature of moral principles. These examples do not show that such principles are relative. Instead, the defining aspect of positive law proves their absoluteness. Murder and adultery are wrong; no qualifying circumstances or principles justify these acts. But it is critical that these acts be precisely defined by biblical teaching, and in this respect positive law is an important factor.

5

Qualification in Realms of Delegated Authority

Since God has not legislated in every area of life where a decision must be made, man has liberty to choose in these matters. Within this area of expedience is the divine principle of structured authority in human relations. Though each person enjoys individual freedom in questions about human judgment, in another sense no one is exempt from the obligation to follow the directions of certain leaders in given social realms. God has given these persons the right to make decisions for others who, in turn, have the responsibility to submit to those decisions. Man's freedom in the area of expedience is to be understood in this restricted sense.

In His infinite wisdom God instituted the principle of organization in human relations to provide social order. Without this God-ordained element in society, mankind would be in a state of chaotic anarchy. The inevitable tension between opposing wills would lead to unbearable turmoil. If unrest in society exists in the presence of structured authority, imagine the condition of the world in the absence of such governance! The only way for this friction to be relieved is for one side to "give," and God has decreed that all men at some time and in given areas of life encounter this humbling principle.

Perhaps the necessity of social authority is best seen by way of contrast in a familiar Old Testament verse: "In those days there was no king in Israel; everyone did what was right in his own eyes" (Judg. 17:6; 21:25). The condition of Israel during the 450-year period of the judges vividly illustrates the folly of anarchy. Religious apostasy, moral degeneration, and national ruin are recurring themes in this dark age in Israel's history. Only when God's people united under the leadership of the judges did they prosper as a nation.

The Principle of Delegated Authority in Scripture

On the broadest level of social relations, God implemented structure in society by ordaining civil government. The earliest reference in Scripture to this institution as an ordinance of God is Genesis 9:6: "Whoever sheds man's blood, by man his blood shall be shed; for in the image of God He made man." Though the judicial process by which murderers were convicted is not specified in this verse, the authorization for capital punishment is indicated in the short phrase "by man." Because God delegated power over human life in this verse, Leupold maintains that

> . . . if man receives power over other men's lives under certain circumstances, then by virtue of having received power over the highest good that man has, power over lesser things is naturally included, such as power over property to the extent of being able to exact taxes, over our persons to the extent of being able to demand various types of work and service, as need may arise. Government, then, being grounded on this word, is not by human contract, or by surrender of certain powers, or by encroachment of priestcraft. It is a divine institution.[1]

That governing authorities have power delegated by God to punish criminals and exact taxes is particularly clear in the New Testament. "Let every soul be subject to the governing authorities," Paul wrote. "For there is no authority except from God, and the authorities that exist are appointed by God"

[1]H.C. Leupold, *Exposition of Genesis* (Grand Rapids, MI: Baker Book House, 1942), Vol. I, p. 333.

(Rom. 13:1). He instructed Titus to remind Christians "to be subject" to rulers and authorities (Titus 3:1). Peter admonished his readers to submit "to every ordinance of man for the Lord's sake" (I Pet. 2:13). Even the Jews, who enjoyed civil as well as religious independence from other nations in their beginning, were expected to submit to the authority of despised Roman rulers: "Render therefore to Caesar the things that are Caesar's, and to God the things that are God's" (Matt. 22:21). Jesus did not deny the authority Pilate claimed but simply reminded him that this power was given to him from above (John 19:10-11).

Before the ordaining of civil government, however, was the institution of the home. The first pronouncement of a structure of authority in the home occurs after the fall: ". . . your desire shall be for your husband, and he shall rule over you" (Gen. 3:16). But although Eve's sin is one of the reasons given by Paul for woman's subjection to man (I Tim. 2:14), this is not the only reason for her role in the home.

Paul gave as another reason the fact that "Adam was first formed, then Eve" (I Tim. 2:13; cf. I Cor. 11:3, 7-8). The wife's duty to be in subjection to her husband is taught throughout the epistles (Col. 3:18; Eph. 5:22-24) and is not removed when the husband is an unbeliever (I Pet. 3:1-6). Equally as explicit is biblical teaching concerning the responsibility of children to submit to parents: "Children, obey your parents in the Lord, for this is right" (Eph. 6:1). Connected with parental authority is the responsibility to discipline children (Prov. 3:12; I Sam. 3:13), even to the point of corporal punishment (Prov. 22:15; 23:13-14). The first years of one's life, the critical formative period of personality, is ideally the first encounter with the lesson of respect for authority.

Since congregations are composed of Christians working together for a common cause, God has also placed a structure of authority in the church. Qualified men referred to as elders (I Pet. 5:1), bishops (overseers—I Tim. 3:1; Acts 20:28), or pastors (Eph. 4:11) occupy a divinely ordained role of leadership. As shepherds, these men are to tend the flock (I Pet. 5:2); as bishops, they are to oversee the work to be done (Acts 20:28; I Tim. 3:1). This latter concept indicates the authority that resides in this position. As a result, members have the responsibility to respect and follow their leadership: "Obey those who rule over you, and be submissive, for they watch for your souls, as those who must give account . . ." (Heb. 13:17a). Among the qualifications which fit a man for this work, the fact that he must be "one who rules well his own house" is crucial, because "if a man does not know how to rule his own house, how will he take care of the church of God" (I Tim. 3:4-5)?

In addition to these institutions, the general principle of submission is applied in the Scriptures to specific human relations. Perhaps initially surprising to newly converted servants in the first century was New Testament teaching regarding master-servant relations. Servants were told, "Be obedient to those who are your masters according to the flesh" (Eph. 6:5a). Similar instructions are given throughout the epistles (Col. 3:22-25; Philem. 1:1-25), even in cases where the master is an unbeliever (I Tim. 6:1-2) or is harsh (I Pet. 2:18). Also taught in the new covenant is the submission of the young to the old (I Pet. 5:5), a principle continued from the respect due to elders enjoined in the Old Testament (Lev. 19:32) and based upon the obvious wisdom acquired through experience.

Two other considerations are significant at this point. One is that authority granted by God may in turn be delegated. Parents, for instance, may delegate authority to teachers and guardians, and their children are obligated to be in subjection to these overseers (Gal. 3:24-25; 4:1-2). This is to be distinguished from shifting responsibility, a prerogative parents do not have from God.

Another important distinction is that in some instances the duty of submission arises from a voluntary decision while in other areas it does not. While a child does not choose the parents to whom he is to be subject, a woman in entering marriage voluntarily places herself in subjection to her husband. Also, if the free will of servants in New Testament teaching is involved in their relationship to their masters (Philem. 1:1-25; Col. 3:22-24; Eph. 6:5-8), then those today who accept a position of labor voluntarily place themselves in submission to superiors.

Primarily because of the relativism so prevalent in this age, several attempts have been made to weaken the meaning of submission in regard to delegated authority. Feminist movements have vigorously attacked New Testament teaching on the role of women, while others affected by this trend have made pseudo-scholarly attempts to reinterpret biblical teaching on the headship of the husband. This latter approach strips the husband of any decision-making authority and makes marriage a two-person democracy.[2] Others have tried to demote the eldership to a position of "authority-by-example-only."[3] An adequate critique of these views would carry this study beyond its focus.

However, it is worthwhile to mention that the underlying error in both cases is the failure to recognize the broader purposes served by the principle of submission to legitimate human authorities. It is also important to recognize a glaring inconsistency in such reasoning. If the language used in the New Testament to describe these relationships does not involve the concept of decision-making authority in matters of expedience, then parents have no decision-making authority in regard to children and rulers have no authority over citizens,

[2]Paul H. Jewett, *Man as Male and Female* (Grand Rapids, MI: William B. Eerdmans Publishing Company, 1975)); cf. the ideas of "mutual submission" and the husband as "loving servant-leader" (only) in H. Norman Wright, *Before You Remarry* (Eugene, OR: Harvest House Publishers, 1988), pp. 53, 56 and the panel discussion (tape) of the 1991 David Lipscomb University Lectureship "Family of Families."

[3]Jack P. Lewis, *Leadership Questions Confronting the Church* (Nashville, TN: Christian Communications, 1985), pp. 9-41; Flavil B. Yeakley, Jr. *Church Leadership and Organization* (Nashville, TN: Christian Communications, 1986), pp. 17-30; Waymon D. Miller, "The Authority of Elders" in *Studies in Hebrews,* Dub McClish, ed. (Denton, TX: Valid Publications, 1983), pp. 435-448.

since the Bible employs equally as pointed terminology in describing the submission due in these areas (Luke 2:51; Rom. 13:1).

Delegated Authority—Qualified Authority

The authority in the areas just discussed, particularly the home, the church, and civil government, is confined to matters of expedience. It does not pertain to matters concerning which God has already given legislation in His revealed will. While leaders in these realms have authority from God, this prerogative does not extend to altering the teaching of Scripture. This limitation in regard to the type of authority possessed by these leaders is established by several considerations.

What other type of authority could be given in these realms? Since matters of obligation to God have already been decided upon in Scripture, the only questions requiring decision-making authority are those in the area of expedience. To argue otherwise is to make the Bible a non-essential revelation.

The Bible also indicates this restriction in delegated authority by using qualifying phrases. Children are to obey their parents "in the Lord" (Eph. 6:1). Servants are to be subject to those who are their masters "according to the flesh" (Eph. 6:5). Wives are to submit to husbands "as is fitting in the Lord" (Col. 3:18). Christians are to recognize those who are over them "in the Lord" (I Thess. 5:12).

Submission to delegated authorities is thus qualified in terms of the type of decision-making power under consideration. The restrictive phrases in these commands let those in submissive roles know that they are not obligated to obey leaders who instruct them to violate the will of God. No breaking of the duty to submit to delegated authorities occurs in such situations because the passages enjoining this submission are inapplicable in these cases.

Instructions addressed to leaders in these areas also contain restrictive warnings. While children are to be subject to parents, fathers are warned, "Do not provoke your children to wrath" (Eph. 6:4). Masters are to "give up threatening" (Eph. 6:9), husbands are to "love their own wives as their own bodies" (Eph. 5:28), and elders are not to be "lords" over the church (I Pet. 5:3).

The limitation of delegated authority is most clearly shown in qualifying examples in both the Old and New Testament. Shadrach, Meshach, and Abed-Nego were cast into a furnace of fire for refusing to obey King Nebuchadnezzar's decree to worship the golden image (Dan. 3). This is a clear instance of disobeying civil authorities, as is Daniel's refusal to cease praying in spite of the decree of Darius (Dan. 6). Even more pointed is the apostolic example in the face of a council edict that prohibited evangelism. Peter and the other apostles defied this order in the familiar response: "We ought to obey God rather than men" (Acts 5:29). Their action established an important precedent for Christians in succeeding generations when Christianity became an illegal religion in Roman society. It also provides authorization for evangelism today in the face of oppressive governments as well as encouragement for those engaged in this sacrificial and dangerous task.

But upon what basis is the apostles' action justified? Geisler suggests that the command to preach the gospel is "a higher duty than the one to obey government"[4]; Jackson asserts that the apostles "had a greater obligation to a higher power."[5] The appeal to a higher/lower law distinction, however, is irrelevant and unnecessary in justifying the apostles' action. The claim that their defense was justified because God's law is higher than man's law ignores the fact that obedience to rulers is part of the law of God. The basis for this qualification is not that preaching the gospel takes precedence over submission to civil authorities; it is that this submission as a divine duty only

[4]Norman L. Geisler, *Christian Ethics: Options and Issues* (Grand Rapids, MI: Baker Book House, 1989), p. 121.

[5]Wayne Jackson, "The Christian and Government," *Is There a Universal Code of Ethics?* Jim E. Waldron, ed. (Winona, MS: World Literature Fund, 1982), p. 299.

applies to matters of expedience. Rulers have no right to contest any item of divine legislation. When they do so, they have overstepped the bounds of delegated authority. As long as they operate within the confines of this realm, they function as agents of God. When citizens rebel against rulers who exercise this authority legitimately, they "resist the ordinance of God" (Rom. 13:1). The reason "God" and "men" are contrasted in Acts 5:29 is that these civil rulers, having left their rightful area of power, were no longer acting by the authority delegated to them. The apostles' action thus establishes an important qualification of the duty to submit to civil government.

This apostolic example also furnishes valuable information regarding universal statements in Scripture. Peter, for instance, commanded his readers to submit to "every ordinance of man" (I Pet. 2:13). "Every ordinance" in this verse, in light of the considerations already discussed, must mean *every ordinance in the realm of expedient matters pertaining to civil relations.* *Every* in this case does mean "every"; it is misleading to say that *all* sometimes means less than "all" when the word is used in the same sense in both instances. The limitation arises from the fact that a certain type of ordinance is under consideration. *Every* retains its universal force, but the category of things it describes must be determined. The same principle is at work in Paul's admonition for children to obey parents and for servants to obey masters "in all things" (Col. 3:20, 22). The key to harmonizing these verses with other Bible teaching is not to modify the meaning of *all* but to precisely define the category of things to which it refers.

Delegated authority, then, is qualified in a vertical direction by the revealed will of God in Scripture. It is also qualified in a horizontal direction because of the relationship between the different realms in which it resides. The home, the church, and civil government each have been delegated decision-making power in their respective realms of function. Parents have authority over their own children but not over children as a whole in society. Elders make decisions connected with the life and work of the church, but they have no such authority about the internal affairs of the homes of which Christians are also members. Ideally, civil government maintains order and peace in society as a whole without usurping the role of either the home or the church. Of course, the relationship between these realms has been simplified; the moral complexities associated with government intrusions into private matters are too numerous to discuss here. However, the fact remains that a separateness is to exist between these realms of delegated authority. Otherwise, biblical injunctions regarding submission in separate areas are meaningless. Even more important is the fact that an understanding of the distinction between these realms provides a general framework for evaluating difficult decisions.

The principle of submission to delegated authority generates a disposition that is foundational to Christianity: the renouncing of one's own will to follow the will of another. The duty to obey those in positions of authority is a responsibility to God, so that in obeying or disobeying these people one is obeying or disobeying God. It is also true that submission to certain persons on earth is broadly analogous to subjection to the Lord Himself. In terms of practical importance, however, the principle of submission creates a humble attitude of obedience so basic in pleasing God, an attitude often described in the Bible as the heart of a child (Matt. 18:1-4; I Cor. 14:20).

6

Qualification by
Priority of Principle

Jesus and the Sabbath Labor Law

Old Testament teaching on the Sabbath day was quite direct. The fourth of the Ten Commandments required the Israelites to:

> Remember the Sabbath day, to keep it holy. Six days you shall labor and do all your work, but the seventh day is the Sabbath of the Lord your God. In it you shall do no work: you, nor your son, nor your daughter, nor your manservant, nor your maidservant, nor your cattle, nor your stranger who is within your gates. For in six days the Lord made the heavens and the earth, the sea, and all that is in them, and rested the seventh day. Therefore the Lord blessed the Sabbath day and hallowed it (Exod. 20:8-11).

This commanded day of rest was to be observed at all seasons: "Six days you shall work, but on the seventh day you shall rest; in plowing time and in harvest you shall rest" (Exod. 34:21). Details concerning the application of the Sabbath labor law were also given to the Israelites. Moses commanded, "You shall kindle no fire throughout your habitations on the Sabbath day" (Exod. 35:3). Nehemiah reproved the Jews for laboring and trading on the Sabbath:

> In those days I saw in Judah some people treading wine
> presses on the Sabbath, and bringing in sheaves, and
> loading donkeys with wine, grapes, figs, and all kinds of
> burdens, which they brought into Jerusalem on the
> Sabbath day. And I warned them about the day on which
> they were selling provisions (Neh. 13:15).

Though their motives were hypocritical, the Israelites knew
that market trade was forbidden on the Sabbath (Amos 8:5).
Also, Jeremiah specified that they were not to bear a burden
out of their houses or into the gates of Jerusalem on the
Sabbath (Jer. 17:19-27).

So grievous was the violating of the Sabbath labor law that
the death penalty was commanded as punishment for its violation. Moses wrote, "Whoever does any work on it shall be put
to death" (Exod. 35:2). This prohibition was not an idle threat:
a man found gathering sticks on the Sabbath was taken outside the camp and stoned (Num. 15:32-36). God demanded that
the observance of the Sabbath be strictly enforced.

Though the Jews had become lax in their observance of the
Sabbath labor law before and shortly after the Babylonian
exile, their attitude toward this legislation eventually drifted to
the opposite extreme. The rapid spread of Greek culture led the
Jews to intensify efforts to preserve their religious heritage.
While some led revolts against the forces of Gentile domination, a group known as the *Chasidim*, "the pious ones," arose
in the second century B.C. to protect the religious interests of
the Jews. This group was so concerned with resisting the
influence of Greek culture that they overreacted, espousing
radical doctrinal views and establishing themselves as the fore-
runners of the Pharisees of New Testament times. Connected
with this fanaticism was the rabbinical view of oral tradition:
the belief that Moses also instituted oral law as part of the
Jew's religion, with this law consisting of the traditional interpretations of the rabbis.

The Mishnah, a second-century A.D. compilation of earlier
rabbinical views, records examples of the extreme to which the

Sabbath labor law was viewed by the rabbis:

> [He is culpable] that takes out rope enough to make a
> handle for a basket . . .

> [He is culpable] that takes out leather enough to make
> an amulet, or vellum enough to write on it the shortest
> passage in the phylacteries, namely, *Hear, O Israel* . . . ;
> or ink enough to write two letters, or eye-paint enough to
> paint one eye.

> If a man took out a loaf into the public domain he is
> culpable; if two men took it out they are not culpable.

> If a man removed his finger-nails by means of his nails or
> his teeth, and so, too, if [he pulled out] the hair of his
> head, or his moustache or his beard; and so, too, if a
> woman dressed her hair or painted her eyelids or red-
> dened [her face]—such a one R. Eliezer declares liable
> [to a sin-offering]; but the Sages forbid [acts the like of
> these only] by virtue of the [rabbinically ordained] Sab-
> bath rest.

> He is culpable that writes two letters, whether with his
> right hand or with his left, whether the same or different
> letters, whether in different inks or in any language.

> A man may fold up his garments [that he wears on the
> Sabbath] as many as four or five times. Beds may be
> spread on the night of Sabbath for the Sabbath day, but
> not on the Sabbath for the night following the Sabbath.

> A man may not shift about the straw on the bed with his
> hand but he may shift it about with his body.

> If a man's hand or foot is dislocated he may not pour cold
> water over it, but he may wash it after his usual fashion.[1]

Extremism in rabbinical interpretations of the Sabbath labor laws resulted in frequent controversies between Jesus and
the scribes and Pharisees. The ruler of a synagogue, displeased
with Jesus' healing of an infirmed woman on the Sabbath,

[1]Herbert Danby, trans., *The Mishnah* (New York, NY: Oxford University
Press, 1933), *Shabbath* S.2, S.3, 10.5, 10.6, 12.3, 15.3, 20.5, 22.6, pp. 100-121.

protested to the crowd, "There are six days on which men ought to work; therefore come and be healed on them, and not on the Sabbath day" (Luke 13:14). After Jesus healed a lame man, the Jews said, "It is the Sabbath; it is not lawful for you to carry your bed" (John 5:10). When the disciples plucked and ate grain on the Sabbath, the Pharisees asked, "Why are you doing what is not lawful to do on the Sabbath" (Luke 6:2)?

Jesus' response to these charges exposed the hypocrisy of the Pharisees and their mishandling of the law. In the process, He demonstrated the principal of qualification in regard to the Sabbath. His defense of the disciples in the case of plucking grain on the Sabbath is the most detailed example of an appeal to qualification in the New Testament. Though recorded by Mark (2:23-28) and Luke (6:1-5), Matthew's account is the most thorough of the three:

> At that time Jesus went through the grain fields on the Sabbath. And his disciples were hungry, and began to pluck heads of grain and to eat. But when the Pharisees saw it, they said to Him, "Look, Your disciples are doing what is not lawful to do on the Sabbath!" Then He said to them, "Have you not read what David did when he was hungry, he and those who were with him: how he entered the house of God and ate the showbread which was not lawful for him to eat, nor for those who were with him, but only for the priests? Or have you not read in the law that on the Sabbath the priests in the temple profane the Sabbath, and are blameless? But I say to you that in this place there is One greater than the temple. But if you had known what this means, I desire mercy and not sacrifice you would not have condemned the guiltless. For the Son of Man is Lord even of the Sabbath" (Matt. 12:1-8).

In keeping with their hair-splitting traditions, the Pharisees viewed the disciples' act of "plucking" heads of grain and "rubbing them in their hands" (Luke 6:1) as a violation of the Sabbath labor law. As Jesus' defense shows, they were guilty themselves of "condemning the guiltless." Extending the application of the Sabbath restrictions beyond the boundaries of their original purpose, the Pharisees tried to make these restrictions address situations they were not intended by God to address. Their mistake was an overapplication of one of God's laws. The innocence of the disciples, then, is clearly stated by Jesus.

But how did Jesus prove their innocence? More specifically, how did He show that their act of plucking grain was not the "labor" the Sabbath law prohibited? What were the boundaries of this law? These questions go beyond the interests of the Pharisees, whose approach was insincere to begin with and whose methods were inconsistent. A sincere, pious Old Testament Israelite would naturally wonder which types of physical activity were included in the Sabbath work prohibition and which were not.

Jesus' first line of reasoning to vindicate the disciples was the example of David and his men in their eating the showbread. The showbread in the temple was replaced each Sabbath, with the old showbread being eaten by the priests (Lev. 24:5-8; I Sam. 21:6). This story, recorded in I Samuel 21, occurred while David was being pursued by Saul. Jesus adds that David and his men were hungry when they asked for the showbread. David's act of eating the showbread has been the subject of much misinterpretation.

Joseph Fletcher in his situational ethics approach argues that David broke the showbread ordinance but holds that David's actions were justified on the basis of "love."[2] Geisler, who does not subscribe to Fletcher's theory, nevertheless takes the same approach to this case, asserting that David literally broke the law but was excused on the basis of human need.[3] Others seeking to avoid the relativism of Fletcher, argue that David literally broke the showbread restriction but assert that Jesus was not trying to justify David's actions. Coffman contends

[2]Joseph Fletcher, *Situation Ethics: The New Morality* (Philadelphia, PA: The Westminster Press, 1966), p. 85.

[3]Norman L. Geisler and Paul D. Feinberg, *Introduction to Philosophy: A Christian Perspective* (Grand Rapids, MI: Baker Book House, 1980), p. 416.

that "the Pharisees wholeheartedly approved of that far more flagrant case of sabbath-breaking by David (for David's action *was* unlawful; the disciples' was not), and yet were willing to press an accusation of wrong-doing against the Christ for something of infinitely less consequence."[4] According to Coffman and others,[5] Jesus charged the Pharisees with the inconsistency of condemning His disciples for plucking grain on the Sabbath while condoning David's eating of the showbread.

The main problem with saying that David actually sinned in eating the showbread is the connection Jesus makes between this action and the actions of the priests on the Sabbath (Matt. 12:5). Matthew's account alone records the example of the priests' Sabbath labor. The conjunction *or* connects the two examples; it indicates a parallel,[6] not a contrast, in reasoning. In response to the Pharisees' unjust charge, Jesus asks, "Have you not read what David did . . . Or have you not read in the law that on the Sabbath the priests in the temple profane the Sabbath, and are blameless?" The connective *or* indicates that both examples are in the same category as far as right and wrong are concerned. Jesus cites the case of David for the same

[4]James Burton Coffman, *Commentary on the Gospel of Matthew* (Austin, TX: Firm Foundation Publishing House, 1968), p. 164.

[5]H. A. Dobbs, "Problem Passages," *The Firm Foundation* (Austin, TX: Firm Foundation Publishing House, 1985), September 24, 1985, pp. 5-6; Dan Winkler, "Does David's Eating the Showbread Teach Situation Ethics?", *Difficult Texts of the New Testament Explained,* Wendell Winkler, ed. (Hurst, TX: Winkler Publications, 1981), p. 102; J. W. McGarvey, *The New Testament Commentary: Matthew and Mark* (Des Moines, Iowa: Eugene S. Smith, 1875), pp. 103-104. In his joint work with Pendleton, however, McGarvey seems to modify his position on David's actions--J. W. McGarvey and Philip Y. Pendleton, *The Fourfold Gospel* (Cincinnati, OH: Standard Publishing), pp. 209-213.

[6]The particle *e* (or) in Matthew 12:5 is used "to introduce a question which is parallel to a preceding one or supplements it . . . *have you not read . . . ? Or have you not read . . . ?* Mt. 12(3), 5 . . ." (William F. Arndt and F. Wilbur Gingrich, *A Greek-English Lexicon of the New Testament and Other Early Christian Literature* [Chicago: University of Chicago Press, 1957], p. 342.)

reason that He appeals to the example of the priests—to justify the actions of the disciples.

The position that David actually sinned misses the point in Jesus' reasoning. Why would Jesus attempt to justify a right action by citing a case of wrongdoing? This strained interpretation merely creates confusion. It has Jesus defending a right action by appealing to an example of wrong-doing and to an example of justified action when both examples are part of the same argumentation! Aside from the fact that the connective *or* will not allow this interpretation, this view of Jesus' reasoning fails to recognize the design of Jesus' response.

But why then did Jesus say that David's eating of the showbread was "not lawful"? Is this not a plain indication that David did actually break the law? This question cannot be adequately examined without raising the same question in regard to the word *profane* in verse 5. When Jesus said that "on the Sabbath the priests in the temple profane the sabbath," did He mean that the priests literally, actually profaned the Sabbath? God Himself commanded the priests to perform the necessary labor in the temple on the Sabbath:

> And on the Sabbath day two lambs in their first year, without blemish, and two-tenths of an epah of fine flour as a grain offering, mixed with oil, with its drink offering—this is the burnt offering for every Sabbath, besides the regular burnt offering with its drink offering (Num. 28:9-10).

The preparation and cleaning involved in these prescribed offerings amounted to physical labor. This activity on the Sabbath could not have been sinful since it was commanded by God. But Jesus said the priests "profaned" the Sabbath in performing this service. This word is used by Jesus in an accommodative sense and means that the priests seemingly or apparently profaned the Sabbath. Applying the Pharisees' reasoning to the priests, Jesus shows the absurdity of their charge against the disciples. According to the Pharisees' reasoning, the priests "profaned" the Sabbath. But they could not literally violate the Sabbath by doing what God had commanded; they could not literally profane the Sabbath and be literally blameless in the same act. The word *profane,* then, must be understood in a non-literal sense. Since the profaning of the Sabbath by the priests is parallel (by virtue of the connective *or*) to the actions of David, the words *not lawful* also must be understood in this accommodative sense. David did that "which was not lawful" in the same sense that the priests "profaned" the Sabbath: a seeming or apparent, not an actual and literal sense. Christ "broke the Sabbath" in the same sense (John 5:18).

While not supporting the extreme of situational ethics as advocated by Fletcher, Jesus' defense of the disciples does provide significant details about the principle of qualification. Each of the three approved actions in Matthew 12:1-8 (the disciples' plucking of grain, David's eating of the showbread, and the priests' labor on the Sabbath) was a qualification of a general prohibition. In the case of the priests, the command to perform temple services qualified the Sabbath work restriction. God forbade the Israelites to work on the Sabbath yet commanded the priests to work on this day. Two types of work were under consideration—one acceptable, and the other unacceptable. The labor of the priests was not included in the category of actions denoted by the word *work* in Exodus 20:10. The labor forbidden on the Sabbath in the Ten Commandments is the type of work commanded on the other six days of the week: physical labor for the purpose of personal and family livelihood. The Pharisees did not consider this qualification of the Sabbath law when they accused the disciples. They did, however, admit some qualifications of the Sabbath law.

Traditional rabbinical teaching as recorded in the Mishnah permitted circumcision on the Sabbath.[7] The New Testament records this allowance, and Jesus used it as an occasion to show the inconsistency of the Jews:

[7]"They may perform on the Sabbath all things that are needful for circumcision . . ." (Shabbath XIX, 2). "R. Jose says: Great is circumcision which overrides even the rigour of the Sabbath" (Nedarim III, 11).

> Moses therefore gave you circumcision (not that it is from Moses, but from the fathers), and you circumcise a man on the Sabbath. If a man receives circumcision on the Sabbath, so that the law of Moses should not be broken, are you angry with Me because I made a man completely well on the Sabbath (John 7:22-23)?

The law of Moses commanded circumcision on the eighth day (Lev. 12:3). What if the eighth day fell on the Sabbath? The Sabbath law prohibited work on the seventh day of the week, but the law of circumcision in some situations required this operation on the Sabbath. Which law "overrides" the other in this apparent conflict? The Jews had rightly concluded that the law of circumcision qualified the Sabbath work prohibition. The physical activity involved in circumcision was not the type of work prohibited by the Sabbath law. The Jews were hypocritical, however, in condemning Jesus for healing on the Sabbath while they performed circumcision on the same day.

The Jews even considered taking care of their livestock to be a qualification of the Sabbath law. In an emergency such as a sheep that had fallen into a pit, the Jews did not hesitate to pull it out (Matt. 12:11). But this activity on the animal's behalf extended to daily provisions: "Does not each one of you on the Sabbath loose his ox or his donkey from the stall, and lead it away to water it" (Luke 13:15)?

In each of these references, Jesus is responding to the Jews' charge that healing on the Sabbath was forbidden. If the Jews both saved and sustained the life of their animals on the Sabbath, how could they condemn Jesus for healing human beings on the Sabbath? "Of how much more value then is a man than a sheep" (Matt. 12:12)? Jesus did not directly affirm that the physical activity expended in caring for these animals was justified. He refers to these actions simply to show the inconsistency of the Jews. However, these actions were permitted by the law of Moses. When Jesus said that man has "more value" than animals, He indicates that animal life does have some degree of value. In fact, the Mosaic law taught the Jews to respect animal life, not tolerating the mistreatment of this part of God's creation (Exod. 23:12, 19; Deut. 22:6-7; 25:4; Prov. 12:10). This principle seems to qualify the Sabbath restriction, allowing the Jews to save or sustain the life of their livestock.

The case of David is a unique aspect in Jesus' defense of the disciples. His eating of the showbread was unlike the actions of the priests in that it was not a qualification of the Sabbath labor law. Instead, this action involved a qualification of the ordinance which required used showbread to be given to the priests (Lev. 24:5-9). His example is also different from the case of the disciples in this respect. The qualifying principle behind the actions of David and the actions of the disciples, however, is the same. The point of similarity in both cases was human need—both David and the disciples acted out of hunger (Matt. 12:1, 3). The primacy of human need qualified both the Sabbath labor restriction and the showbread ordinance; the principle of benevolence qualified the positive requirements of worship.

Jesus' explanation of the relationship between these apparently conflicting laws clarifies the proper application of the principle of qualification for readers of the New Testament. But what about Jews living prior to the time of Christ? How could those without His explanation determine what was and what was not a legitimate qualification of divine law? Jesus' criticism of the Pharisees implies not only that they could have inferred these qualifications but that they were expected by God to do so. What information in the law should have enabled them to recognize that the disciples' actions were not a violation of the Sabbath? Jesus shows that the example of David and the case of the priests should have sufficed, asking, "Have you not read . . . ?" One passage in the law in particular had been ignored by the Pharisees. Had the Pharisees known the meaning of the words "I desire mercy and not sacrifice" (Hos. 6:6), they would not have "condemned the guiltless" (Matt. 12:7). From this principle the Pharisees should have concluded that the actions of the disciples were justified. Jesus had earlier exhorted a group of Pharisees to learn the meaning of Hosea's words after they had criticized Him for eating with tax collectors and sinners (Matt. 9:13).

What, then, is the meaning of Hosea's statement and what is the relationship of the principle contained in it to other commands in the law? The answers to these questions demands a close analysis of the verse itself. *Mercy* in Hosea 6:6 is used in the general sense of being merciful to others, of being compassionate toward the needs of one's neighbor. This meaning is particularly evident in Jesus' application of the Hosea passage in Matthew. The negation in the statement, "I desire mercy and not sacrifice," cannot mean that God did not in any sense desire sacrifice (with *sacrifice* standing for the positive requirements of worship in general). Since God did require the Jews to worship, the negation must be understood in a comparative, not an absolute, sense. The negative is sometimes used, not to absolutely cancel the word to which it applies, but to emphasize the part of the sentence being affirmed. "You have not lied to men but to God" (Acts 5:4) does not deny what had just occurred (Ananias' lie to Peter). It does, however, emphasize that Ananias lied primarily to God. He lied to Peter, but he lied especially to God; he lied not so much to men as he did to God.[8] The same emphasis occurs in I Thessalonians 4:8 ("he who rejects this does not reject man, but God"). Similarly, "I desire mercy and not sacrifice" places special emphasis on the virtue of mercy.

Because of their failure to understand Hosea's words, the Pharisees were unjustly critical of Jesus' disciples. But their

[8]The interpretation "You have not (only) lied to men but (also) to God" weakens the emphatic aspect of Peter's words, while Meyer's view "You have not (at all) lied to men but (only) to God" is overly literal (H. A. W. Meyer, *Critical and Exegetical Handbook to the Acts of the Apostles* [Peabody, MA: Hendrickson Publishers, 1983 reprint], p. 106). Winer follows Meyers' reasoning but admits that the negative is sometimes used "not for the purpose of really (logically) canceling the first conception, but in order to direct undivided attention to the second, so that the first may comparatively disappear" (George Benedict Winer, *A Grammar Idiom of the New Testament* [Andover: Warren F. Draper, 1886], p. 497).

overapplication of the Sabbath restriction did not result from an innocent misunderstanding of a single Old Testament verse. They had instead failed on a much broader scale by not appreciating one of the fundamental themes of the law. The divine wish expressed in Hosea merely summarizes a principle at the very heart of the Old Testament: the preeminence of love for one's neighbor. With emphasis on this topic being absent in the life and teaching of the Pharisees, one of the primary concerns of Jesus was to point the Jews back to the place of this theme in the law. In Jesus' words, "This is the Law and the Prophets" (Matt. 7:12). "You shall love your neighbor as yourself" is second in importance only to the command to love God supremely (Mark 12:28-31). When a scribe said that to fulfill these two duties was "more than all the whole burnt offerings and sacrifices," Jesus said to him, "You are not far from the kingdom of God" (Mark 12:33-34). This emphasis is maintained in the epistles, particularly in Paul's reminder that "all the law is fulfilled in one word, even in this: 'You shall love your neighbor as yourself' " (Gal. 5:14). But the Jews should have been able to grasp this theme from a study of the Old Testament alone. Its teaching on this subject is stressed throughout its pages, culminating in Micah's question, "What does the Lord require of you but to do justly, to love mercy, and to walk humbly with your God" (Mic. 6:8)?

As a result of not recognizing this primary theme, the Pharisees were unable to properly relate the individual commands of the law to each other. The law itself, however, had indicated the relative importance of outward observances of worship and compassionate acts of mercy. Solomon wrote that "to do righteousness and justice is more acceptable to the Lord than sacrifice" (Prov. 21:3), with *sacrifice* (as in Hos. 6:6) denoting the positive rites of worship in general. The Old Testament shows that without a corresponding life of justice and mercy, burnt offerings and sacrifices are vain (Amos 5:21-23; Isa. 1:11-17; Mic. 6:6-8).

But Solomon goes further than merely stating that a merciful life is necessary, and so does Jesus. Solomon said that a just and righteous life is "more acceptable" to the Lord than sacrifice. These words echo the declaration of Samuel: "To obey is better than sacrifice" (I Sam. 15:22). Proper worship in the Old Testament was acceptable to the Lord; in fact, it is described as a "sweet aroma" to God (Lev. 1:9). Also, neither Solomon nor Samuel meant that worship was a light matter in God's sight, as the recorded punishments for unauthorized worship show (Lev. 10:1-2; II Sam. 6:1-8). Their words stress that a benevolent life is more primary in the sight of God than offerings and sacrifices. This is the significance of the expression "I desire mercy and not sacrifice" as cited by Jesus in Matthew 12. Though this saying was originally spoken by Hosea as a rebuke of deliberate acts of sin among God's people (Hos. 6:6-10), Jesus' application of it shows that mercy includes the benevolent attitude of allowing the hungry to eat.

A distinction should be observed between the qualification of the Sabbath law in the case of the priests and the qualification of the showbread ordinance in the case of David. In the example of the priests, the qualification arose out of an explicit positive command of God. The work prohibition in Exodus 20:10 did not apply to the duties performed by the priests on the Sabbath because God Himself authorized this work. Had God meant by the word *work* in Exodus 20:10 any physical activity, He would not have commanded the services recorded in Numbers 28:9-10. In both the case of David and of Jesus' disciples, however, the type of qualification at work is an overriding principle, not an express command. The "dilemma" in David's situation was that the showbread was to be given to the priests, yet David and his men were hungry and the showbread was the only food available. The principle of mercy, which involves supply of basic human needs, qualified the ordinance regarding the showbread.

Modern examples of this type of qualification are not difficult to find. For instance, Christians are commanded to assemble for worship on the first day of the week (I Cor. 11:17-34; 14:26-40; 16:1-2). But what if a Christian, driving to worship, witnesses an accident in which several people are critically injured? What if this Christian was the only person present to save the lives of those injured? Should he choose not to assemble with the saints and try to save their lives or should he assemble for worship, leaving the victims of the accident to suffer and perhaps die?

In a similar incident, suppose that just prior to the time to leave home and travel to the place of worship a family member is severely injured in a fall. Is at least one other person in the family justified in not assembling for worship to care for the injured loved one?

Closer to the case of David in I Samuel 21, suppose that an impoverished congregation in a remote mission area has assembled for worship. An abandoned and desperate mother and her five small children wander into the assembly, begging for help. At the point of starvation, she asks for food, and the only food available is the elements of the communion. Would the congregation be justified in feeding this starving family when none of the communion elements will be left for the Lord's Supper? The usual response is that the proper course of action is obvious—in these situations, the demands of worship give way to human need.

But what is the basis for this choice? Strange as the question may sound, how do we know that God desires one action in these examples rather than the other since He seems to command both? Unless the biblical principle of qualification involved is clearly identified, the Christian will have no biblical guidelines in similar but less obvious circumstances.

The qualifying principle at work in David's case and in the examples above is the fact that some matters of biblical teaching have a priority of importance in terms of their relation to other divine requirements. These items of divine legislation take precedence in cases in which duties required by God seem to conflict. This priority of importance is taught in Hosea 6:6, but it is specifically expressed in Jesus' observation that justice, mercy, and faith are "weightier matters of the law" (Matt. 23:23).[9] The qualification exerted by such matters is described in terms of higher/lower law distinction[10] or as graded absolutism.[11] Other items of biblical legislation must be interpreted in light of these weightier precepts. Simply put, God did not design the Sabbath law or the showbread ordinance to keep back food from legitimate cases of hunger.

Corban and the Fifth Commandment

A similar encounter between Jesus and the Pharisees illustrates the pettiness of first century rabbinic theology. This confrontation, recorded by Matthew (15:1-11) and Mark (7:1-16), began when the Pharisees "saw some of His disciples eat bread with defiled, that is, with unwashed hands" (Mark 7:2). The critics did not claim that the disciples had violated the law of Moses; they instead charged them with transgressing "the tradition of the elders" (Matt. 15:2). Their hypersensitivity to Gentile influences had given rise to a radical view of ceremonial cleanness. As Mark observes, "When they come from the marketplace, they do not eat unless they wash" (Mark 7:4a). This paranoia about uncleanness extended even to the point of washing household utensils and furniture (Mark 7:4b).

Jesus later explained to the multitude that "the things which come out of him, those are the things that defile a man" (Mark 7:15), not the particles of dirt that may enter the body through eating with unwashed hands. In His initial response, however, Jesus countered the Pharisees' accusation with a more serious

[9]"Weightier" is from *barus* used here in the comparative form and denoting "the more important provisions of the law" (William F. Arndt and F. Wilbur Gingrich, *A Greek-English Lexicon of the New Testament and Other Early Christian Literature* [Chicago: University of Chicago Press, 1958], p. 134).

[10]J. W. McGarvey and Philip Y. Pendleton, *The Fourfold Gospel* (Cincinnati, OH: Standard Publishing), p. 213.

[11]Norman L. Geisler, *Christian Ethics: Options and Issues* (Grand Rapids, MI: Baker Book House, 1989), pp. 113-132.

charge. The Pharisees complained that the disciples had broken tradition; Jesus rebuked them for violating the law of God:

> All too well you reject the commandment of God, that you may keep your tradition. For Moses said, "Honor your father and your mother"; and, "He who curses father or mother, let him be put to death." But you say, "If a man says to his father or mother, 'Whatsoever profit you might have received from me is Corban (that is, dedicated to the temple)'; and you no longer let him do anything for his father or his mother, making the word of God of no effect through your tradition which you have handed down" (Mark 7:9-13a).

Matthew's record of this tradition is "Whoever says to his father or mother, 'Whatever profit you might have received from me has been dedicated to the temple'—is released from honoring his father or mother" (Matt. 15:5-6). Because of their insistence on such man-made doctrines, the worship which the Pharisees offered to God was vain (Matt. 15:9; cf. Isa. 29:13).

The *Corban* tradition, apparently an established practice in Jesus' time, is also mentioned by Josephus[12] and is thoroughly illustrated in the Mishnah.[13] The word *Corban* and its substitutes *Conam, Conah,* and *Conas* were used in declaring vows that set apart objects for sacred use. The Jews held that property that had been dedicated to God by a vow could not be used to benefit anyone else. The tractate *Nedarim* (vows) in the Mishnah sets forth the extent to which such pronouncements were to be kept:

> . . . If a man said, "May what I eat of thine be the *Korban*"; or "as a *Korban*" or "*a Korban*," it is forbidden to him.

[12]Josephus describes Corban as an "oath" which "can only be found among the Jews, and declares what a man may call 'a thing devoted to God'"—Flavius Josephus, *Against Apion,* 1.22, *The Works of Josephus,* trans. William Whitson (Lynn, MA: Hendrickson Publishers, 1980), p. 614. Note also *Antiquities,* IV, 4.4.

[13]*The Mishnah,* trans. Herbert Danby (Oxford: Oxford University Press, 1933), pp. 264-280.

... If a man saw others eating [his] figs and said, "May they be *Korban* to you!" And they were found to be his father and brothers and others with them, the School of Shammai say: For them the vow is not binding, but for the others with them it is binding. And the School of Hillel say: The vow is binding for neither of them.

[If a man said] ... "Let this cloak be *Korban* so long as it is not burnt!" he may not redeem them.

[If a man said to his fellow,] "May I be to thee as a thing that is banned!" he against whom the vow is made is forbidden [to have any benefit from him] ... (*Nedarim* 1.4; 3.2, 5; 5.4).

Further inspection of this section of the Mishnah shows that the leading rabbis were divided as to whether vows could be broken for the sake of meeting obligations to parents:

R. Eliezer says: They may open for man the way [to repentance] by reason of the honour due to father and mother. But the Sages forbid it. R. Zadok said: Rather than open the way for a man by reason of the honour due to father and mother, they should open the way for him by reason of the honour due to God ... (*Nedarim* 9:1).

What should be remembered about rabbinic oral tradition is that its prescribed rules were supposed inferences and applications of the law itself. The rabbis claimed scriptural justification for their views. They were not so bold as to assert these teachings without having some semblance of support from the law. The Pharisees saw these traditions as logical deductions from the law, not as human doctrines. The Corban tradition seems to have had a supposed scriptural basis. In particular, the view that Corban had an overriding effect on the duty to honor one's parents appears to have been based on two concerns: the stringency of vows in the law and the physical support of the public religious life of Israel.

The law did stress the obligatory nature of vows. Moses wrote, "If a man vows a vow to the Lord, or swears an oath to bind himself by some agreement, he shall not break his word;

he shall do according to all that proceeds out of his mouth" (Num. 30:2; cf. Deut. 23:21-23). Solomon later warned, "When you make a vow to God, do not delay to pay it; for he has no pleasure in fools" (Eccles. 5:4a). The Pharisees reasoned that if a man dedicated any of his property to the Lord, his vow could not be superseded even by the needs of his aged parents. This meant that a dedicated house, field, or other type of property could be withheld from needy parents. The Pharisees "no longer let him do anything for his father or his mother" because of a higher allegiance to tradition.

The law had also given the Jews the responsibility of supplying the physical items necessary for public worship. The tabernacle was built through free will offerings (Exod. 35-40), and God later rebuked His people for not rebuilding the battered temple (Hag. 1:2-9). The Aramaic word *Corban* is explained by Mark as "dedicated," from *doron*, a word used for gifts in general (Matt. 2:11) but more often for "sacrificial gifts and offerings" (Matt. 5:23-24; 8:4; Heb. 5:1; 9:9).[14] The words "to the temple" (NKJV) are supplied by the translators, as are the words "to God" in other versions (ASV, RSV, NASB, NRSV, NIV). *Corban* refers to "a gift consecrated to God, to be used for religious purposes."[15] The alleged concern of the Pharisees was the upkeep of the temple as well as commitment to vows. So important was this concern to the Pharisees that they believed it outweighed the obligation to take care of needy parents.

The *Corban* tradition as practiced by the Jews in Jesus' time should not be viewed as an honest mistake of interpretation. While not every rabbi's motives may be impugned, the Mishnah shows indications of deception and selfishness in regard to the *Corban* tradition.

> Men may vow to murderers, robbers, or tax-gatherers that what they have is Heave-offering even though it is not Heave-offering; or that they belong to the king's

---

[14]Arndt and Gingrich, *Greek-English Lexicon*, pp. 210-211.
[15]*Ibid.*, p. 444.

household even though they do not belong to the king's household (Nedarim III,4).

To at least some rabbis, the *Corban* tradition overrode the biblical injunction to be honest.

Also, the Pharisees were covetous men (Luke 16:14) who were rebuked by Jesus for their greed (Matt. 23:14, 16-17), and the chief priests and elders had charge of the temple treasury (Matt. 27:6, *korbannas*). The motives of the religious leaders were not pure. Jesus Himself said, "Their heart is far from me" (Mark 7:6). In addition, the practice of *Corban* became a convenient excuse, a pretense for not supporting ailing parents. A Jewish man may have told his parents that the property was dedicated when he had no intention of offering it. As the Mishnah shows, the *Corban* pronouncement was used for withholding items from use by others when the offerer merely wanted to keep possessions for his own benefit. In practice, this tradition lended itself to the selfish motives among the Jews.

Although the *Corban* tradition was associated with impure motives, Jesus' exposure of it provides important information regarding synthesis of Bible teaching. In particular, His discussion shows that the Jews had failed to incorporate relevant principles in the law in their application of *Corban*. While the stringency of vows and the obligation to support the temple were legitimate principles within their realm of application, the Pharisees' extremism had led to an overapplication of these duties.

Even a general acquaintance with the law, however, would have exposed the Pharisees' unbending view of vows of dedication. The law enabled the Jews to redeem property that had been dedicated (Lev. 27). But aside from this obvious qualification in the law, Jesus' reply to the Pharisees reveals a significant truth: vows, though binding in general, do not override all other considerations in Scripture. The nature of a vow is central to understanding its relationship to biblical obligations. A vow is a *chosen* commitment that creates an obligation to God but does not remove duties already given by Him. For instance, marital vows, once entered, establish new responsibilities in addition to basic obligations still present. Unless vows are understood in this qualified sense, they may be misused to avoid previously given duties. Biblical teaching on the stringency of vows does not grant vows unqualified authority over all other divine obligations. The voluntary *Corban* vow did not override the unchosen responsibility to honor father and mother.

Also, a distinction should be made between divinely authorized and divinely unauthorized vows. Some vows should not be made. If such an unauthorized vow is made, the person making the vow is not obligated to God to keep it. To argue otherwise is to affirm the absurd. If a person vows never to obey God, does God obligate him to keep the vow? The warning in Deuteronomy 23:21-23 does not apply to unauthorized vows. Failure to acknowledge this distinction leads to the mistaken position that all vows are "inviolate."[16] Jesus' response to the Pharisees, however, shows that the principle of honoring one's parents qualifies vows of dedication.

Jesus also shows the relative importance of public offerings for the upkeep of the temple and the duty to provide for father and mother. The term *honor* in this discussion is shown to include benevolence as well as respect. The responsibility of caring for one's parents is the more primary of the duties, qualifying the obligation of supporting the physical maintenance of the temple. God did not intend for the needs of a building for public worship to override such a fundamental responsibility. Though God expected the Jews to provide necessities for the temple, it is misleading to classify this obligation as a duty to God and the responsibility to care for one's parents as a duty to man. Some rabbis had evidently suggested this false dichotomy, arguing that duties to God override duties to men. Caring for one's parents is an obligation owed to God, since it was God who commanded this duty. Passages showing that man's relationship to God takes precedence over man's relationship to others (Deut. 13:6-11; Luke 14:26) do not apply

[16]Norman L. Geisler, *Christian Ethics*, p. 118.

to the supposed tension between temple responsibilities and parental obligations. Both duties arise out of man's accountability to the Creator. In terms of importance, however, duties to parents takes precedence when both obligations cannot be met.

This distinction in benevolent duties establishes a helpful guideline in decision-making concerning giving. The responsibility to provide for the needs of one's immediate family is a central human duty. One who fails to discharge this obligation "is worse than an unbeliever" (I Tim. 5:8). A man has a primary and overriding responsibility to his immediate family members. Having a "natural affection" (Rom. 1:31, KJV) to motivate him to care for his own, he bears a unique relationship to these members. He has obligations to them in a way and to a degree that he does not have to others. The general principle of giving to those outside the home is qualified by this overriding responsibility. When a man has opportunity, he is to do good to all men (Gal. 6:10). But when he cannot both provide for his family and assist legitimate needs outside the home, the duties of this God-ordained institution take precedence. If a poor Jew had enough to feed his family but not enough to feed his family and give to the temple, the responsibility to offer gifts was qualified in his case. The ability to give to needs outside the home is in part determined by the particular needs of the family. Thus, the adage "Charity begins at home" finds support in Jesus' response to the *Corban* tradition.

The similarities between the Sabbath confrontation and the *Corban* discussion point to a broader principle in biblical qualification. Both the Sabbath law and vows of dedication were cases of positive religious observances in Israel. In each case the Jews had overapplied these regulations, failing to acknowledge the qualifying principle Jesus brought to their attention. That basic principle is providing for the physical needs of others. The particular religious requirements of any dispensation do not remove this permanent benevolent principle. Though the required observances of public religious life ought to be done, the "weightier matters of the law" (Matt. 23:23) take precedence over them in cases of apparent conflict.

PART
THREE

APPLICATION

7

Test Cases:
Ethical Problems Examined
in Light of the Principle

The questions discussed in this chapter illustrate the practical need for a closer examination of biblical teaching on qualification. They demonstrate that this area of study is not an ancient theoretical subject with little useful application to modern times. Instead, these examples, covering a wide range of personal problems, show the urgent relevance of this topic to everyday life. Also, these cases expose faulty methods of qualification. It is important to remember that most Bible-believing people appeal to some type of qualification in their approach to these issues. The principle of qualification is often abused in attempts to resolve such matters. The critical question in the following examples is whether the alleged qualifications are biblically supported. It will be necessary at this stage to reassert the principles stated in part two, since the biblical information alone will enable us to determine the proper application of its precepts.

Is Lying Ever Justified?

"You shall not bear false witness against your neighbor" (Exod. 20:16) is one of the most well known verses in the Bible. That lying is morally wrong is virtually universally accepted among the cultures of the world, and the first feelings of the pains of conscience are often the result of a childhood lie. God's attitude toward this sin is found in Solomon's warning that "the Lord hates . . . a lying tongue" (Prov. 6:17). This hatred of lying is reiterated in the New Testament in warnings against this sin (Eph. 4:25; Col. 3:9), in the punishment of Ananias and Sapphira for lying (Acts 5:1-11) and in the sentence of eternal damnation for liars (Rev. 21:8).

Do these verses set forth lying as being wrong without exception, or is lying morally right in some situations because of the qualifying principles involved? In perhaps the most extreme case possible, is it right to lie to save human life, especially when the lives at stake are those in one's immediate family? Does the moral principle of saving human life and the duty to protect one's family qualify the biblical prohibition against lying, making a deliberate falsehood morally right in these circumstances?

Philosophers and theologians since the time of Augustine have written extensively on this problem. Augustine's own view was that lying is unqualifiedly wrong: "A lie is not allowable, even to save another from injury."[1] In the works *On Lying* and *Against Lying* he rigorously defends this view, carefully distinguishing a lie from a joke, a figure of speech, or a concealment of truth from those who would misuse it to hurt another person.[2] This last distinction led Catholics to adopt the phrase "Mental Reservation,"[3] which in its strict sense is seen in the case of Titius who once told a woman that he would take her to wife. When later asked by a judge if he had said this, he replied that he had not because he had no intention of marry-

[1]Augustine, "Enchiridion," XXII, in *A Select Library of the Nicene and Post-Nicene Fathers of the Christian Church*, Philip Schaff, ed. (Grand Rapids, MI: William B. Eerdmans Publishing Company, 1980 reprint), Vol. III, p. 245.

[2]Augustine, "On Lying" and "Against Lying" in *A Select Library of the Nicene and Post-Nicene Fathers of the Christian Church*, Philip Schaff, ed. (Grand Rapids, MI: William B. Eerdmans Publishing Company, 1980 reprint), Vol. III, pp. 455-500.

[3]Walter Dominic Hughes, "Mental Reservation," *New Catholic Encyclopedia* (Washington, D.C.: Catholic University of America, 1967), Vol. IX, p. 662.

ing her when the statement was made. In a broader sense, the doctrine refers to using unclear language to conceal the truth. Aquinas also held that "it is not lawful to tell a lie in order to deliver another from any danger whatever."[4] He did, however, add that "it is lawful to hide the truth prudently, by keeping it back."[5] Kant also held that "a lie is a lie, and is in itself intrinsically base whether it be told with good or bad intent" and "there are no lies which may not be the source of evil."[6]

Dissenting from the position of these influential writers is a group of ethicists who insist that lying to save human life is morally justified. Fletcher, in characteristic situationist fashion, bluntly states that "if love vetoes the truth, so be it."[7] In a section entitled "Compromise and the Limits of Truthfulness,"[8] Thielicke reasons that truth must be understood in view of the end to which it is connected, not merely as factual agreement between a judgment and verifiable facts. He illustrates this allegedly broader concern by pointing out that truth may be misused to achieve a wrong goal just as a falsehood may be used to reach a noble end. Geisler maintains that "the Bible indicates that there are occasions where intentionally falsifying (lying) is justifiable," citing Rahab and the Egyptian midwives as examples of "divinely approved lying to save a life."[9] He even argues that when a person leaves his lights on while away from home, his actions amount to a "lie to save his property from a potential thief."[10]

[4]Thomas Aquinas, *Summa Theologica* IIa IIae 110.3 (Westminster, MD: Christian Classics, 1981 reprint), Vol. III, p. 1661.

[5]*Ibid.*

[6]Immanuel Kant, "Ethical Duties Towards Others: Truthfulness," *Lectures on Ethics,* Louis Infield, trans. (New York, NY: Harper & Row, Publishers, 1963), p. 229.

[7]Joseph Fletcher, *Situation Ethics: The New Morality* (Philadelphia, PA: The Westminster Press, 1966), p. 65.

[8]Helmut Thielicke, *Theological Ethics* (Grand Rapids, MI: William B. Eerdmans Publishing Company, 1984 reprint), pp. 520-566.

[9]Norman L. Geisler, *Christian Ethics: Options and Issues* (Grand Rapids, MI: Baker Book House, 1989), p. 122.

[10]*Ibid.,* p. 94.

An evaluation of the views of these opposing sets of authors should begin with an examination of the biblical material relevant to the question. Since the cases of Rahab and the midwives are offered as evidence that the prohibition against lying is qualified by the weightier principle of mercy, these examples will serve as a starting point. Like many other controversial issues, these matters of consideration are by no means recent. Both Augustine[11] and Aquinas[12] treated such examples in their discussions of lying.

In the case of the midwives (Exod. 1:15-22), the argument of those claiming that this is an example of divinely approved lying is that: (1) Pharaoh commanded the midwives to kill newborn male Hebrews (v. 16); (2) the midwives disobeyed this decree (v. 17); (3) the midwives lied when questioned concerning their actions (vv. 18-19); (4) God blessed the midwives (vv. 20-21); (5) since God blessed the action of which a lie was an integral part, then He must have sanctioned the lie in this circumstance. An assessment of the soundness of this argument must focus on the charge that the midwives lied and the claim that God sanctioned that lie. The actual answer of the midwives to Pharaoh's question, "Why have you done this thing, and saved the male children alive" (Exod. 1:18)? was "Because the Hebrew women are not like the Egyptian women; for they are lively and give birth before the midwives come to them" (Exod. 1:19). Whether their excuse was a statement of biological fact or a lie, the text does not explicitly state.

However, the context indicates that more was involved in the midwives' failure to kill the male infants than what is contained in their answer. Verse 17 indicates a deliberate action on their part, not the suddenness of delivery by Hebrew women: "But the midwives feared God, and did not do as the king of Egypt commanded them, but saved the male children alive." It seems, then, that the midwives did in fact lie. It is a

---

[11]Augustine, "To Consentius: Against Lying," *Nicene and Post-Nicene Fathers,* p. 495-497.

[12]Thomas Aquinas, *Summa Theologica,* IIa IIae, 110.3, p. 1660.

mistake to conclude, however, that God's blessing of the midwives is tantamount to His sanctioning their lie. God blessed them because they feared Him (v. 21), not because they lied.

It is also important to remember that a biblical record of events is often very selective. A considerable time may be summarized in a few verses; this condensed form of a story omits many details. One verse in a short record states the lie of these women. This fact makes the lie more noticeable. If more details were given us regarding the relationship the midwives had with God, perhaps the picture would be easier to solve. All that the record says is that they "feared God"—if this description represents their lives in general, then the place of the lie in this total picture is more easily assessed.

It is possible that the midwives repented of the lie they told and were blessed by God because of their life of godly fear. Their lie may have been an isolated act that was forgiven in the same way as Peter's denial of Christ. The midwives had already engaged in saving the Hebrew children, and their commendable deeds in this regard could have occurred for a significant period of time before they were confronted by Pharaoh. The lie, then, should not be viewed as the inherent reason for God's blessing the midwives.

That Rahab lied concerning the two Israelite spies who came to her house cannot be reasonably doubted. In fact, three lies appear in her response to the king's men: (1) "I did not know where they were from" (Josh. 2:4); (2) "When it was dark . . . the men went out" (v. 5); (3) "Where the men went I do not know" (v. 5). But Rahab is twice cited in the New Testament as an example of faith:

> By faith the harlot Rahab did not perish with those who did not believe, when she had received the spies with peace (Heb. 11:31).

> Likewise, was not Rahab the harlot also justified by works when she received the messengers and sent them out another way (James 2:25)?

The two stated reasons for these commendations of Rahab are that she received the spies (messengers) and that she sent them out another way. Nothing is said about her conversation with the king's men. As in the case of the midwives, this incident should be viewed in light of the overall picture. How much time elapsed from Rahab's reception of the spies to her sending them out is not revealed. It is clear from New Testament commendations that she is being praised for her efforts in general. These later references are not a blanket endorsement of every thought, word, or deed of Rahab during this time. Her lies were not essential parts of the actions commended by James and in Hebrews.[13]

Another point of inquiry about the question of "justified" lying is whether the distinction between some forms of deception and lying can be biblically established. Are all cases of deception lies? Geisler answers yes, arguing that "an intentional deception is a lie."[14] But if every type of deception is a lie, serious implications arise. The battle at Ai (Josh. 8), which Israel fought under the approval of God (vv. 1-2, 7-8, 18-19), was won when Israel mislead her enemy into an ambush. This example is enough to refute Geisler's contention that all deception is lying.

Also, one is not always under obligation to reveal information to an inquirer. God instructed Samuel to reveal a secondary reason for his coming to Bethlehem—to sacrifice to the Lord (I Sam. 16:2)—while allowing him to conceal the primary purpose of his journey—to anoint a new king (v. 1). Since it is impossible for God to lie (Heb. 6:18; Titus 1:2), neither the deception at Ai nor the concealment of fact at Bethlehem could

---

[13]John Murray parallels Rahab's lie and her subsequent deliverance to Jacob and Rebekah's lie and the resulting blessing bestowed by Isaac (*Principles of Conduct*, Eerdmans, 1957, pp. 136-139). Did the fact that Jacob received the blessing justify his lie? While this analogy may be urged in defense of the midwives, the case of Rahab is different in an important respect: Rahab is commended for her faith in the situation described above while Jacob is not.

[14]Geisler, *Christian Ethics*, p. 91.

be inherently evil. This fact concerning the nature of God is fatal to the position that lying is sometimes justified by virtue of the overriding principle of mercy (as in lying to save human life). Since both the prohibition against lying and the principle of mercy are expressions of the nature of God, this alleged qualification has its roots in God. If mercy as an attribute of God is the source of the qualification, then why could not God lie, given Geisler's reasoning, in situations where lying would be the merciful thing to do? If lying is not intrinsically sinful, then why is it impossible for God to lie? In addition to these complications, the God-approved actions at Ai and Bethlehem expose the weakness of Geisler's position by showing that hiding the truth from an attacker by keeping silent is a scriptural alternative.

The essence of the wrongness of lying lies in the state of heart inherent in it. Lying is closely related to stealing in that it involves the same selfish disposition. A liar not only intentionally deceives and falsifies—he does so out of greed and cowardice. Whether a child who lies to avoid punishment or a businessman who lies for profit, all liars share this attitude. Lying has at its roots a desire to benefit only the one guilty of it. It involves an intrinsic opposition to the love of others and renders a spirit of self-denial and sacrifice impossible. A liar perverts truth for selfish gain. He holds back truth to the ultimate hurt of others just as one deprives the hungry of food out of a self-serving outlook.

The absoluteness of the biblical law against lying remains intact in an examination of these points. This negative moral precept is unqualified; there are no situations in which it is right to lie. If, as Geisler claims, this law may be qualified by the principle of mercy, then what about other moral prohibitions? Would he maintain that a homosexual act would be justified if it saved human life? Would adultery be justified if it served the purpose of mercy? Does the principle of mercy have the capacity to override any negative moral law? Virtually everyone "draws the line" at some point; Thielicke himself maintained that there are some principles that cannot be compromised regardless of the situation.[15] From this last question however, emerges a critical distinction in regard to the qualifying force of the principle of mercy. While mercy may qualify positive commands involving the religious and ceremonial observances connected with worship (Matt. 12:1-8), no biblical evidence exists to establish a restriction of moral prohibitions by virtue of the principle of mercy. Thus, mercy cannot transform an immoral act into a moral one. The attempt to justify lying on this basis is an abuse of the principle of qualification.

Unscriptural Marriages and the Demands of Love

Current trends in divorce and remarriage have given rise to the question of whether the principle of qualification plays a part in the application of biblical teaching on this subject. Stringent biblical regulations on remarriage indicate the sacredness of marriage as an institution of God:

> For the woman who has a husband is bound by the law to her husband as long as he lives. But if the husband dies, she is released from the law of her husband. So then if, while her husband lives, she marries another man, she will be called an adulteress; but if her husband dies, she is free from that law, so that she is no adulteress, though she has married another man (Rom. 7:2-3).

> Whoever divorces his wife and marries another commits adultery against her. And if a woman divorces her husband and marries another, she commits adultery (Mark 10:11-12).

> And I say to you, whoever divorces his wife, except for sexual immorality, and marries another commits adultery; and whoever marries her who is divorced commits adultery (Matt. 19:9).

According to New Testament teaching, remarriage is permissible only when one's mate has committed fornication or has

[15]Thielicke, *Theological Ethics*, Vol. I, pp. 643-647.

died. To remarry on any other grounds is to commit adultery.[16]

Today's high rate of divorce has left many in unscriptural remarriages. What is the status of those in such unions? The Bible is clear on this point: those in unauthorized marriages commit adultery. But what about the considerations connected with these unions? Is the declaration of adultery in the teaching of Jesus and Paul qualified by other biblical principles so that what is explicitly called adultery is made legitimate?

Several arguments have been offered in an attempt to establish such qualification. Olan Hicks asserts that divorce and remarriage passages must be interpreted in light of I Corinthians 7:2: "Nevertheless, because of sexual immorality, let each man have his own wife, and let each woman have her own husband."[17] Hicks also stresses Paul's statement regarding the unmarried, "If they cannot exercise self-control, let them marry, for it is better to marry than to burn with passion" (I Cor. 7:9). He argues that human needs are "not changed by the fact that one commits the sin of breaking marriage or sins against his vows or has the misfortune of a mate doing that to him."[18] His conclusion is that unions that violate the passages cited earlier are justified on the basis of the overriding principle of a God-instilled drive for companionship with the opposite sex.[19] Stanley Ellisen adds that the fulfilling of family needs is a legitimatizing factor in the issue of remarriage:

[16]This is one of the most controversial subjects in modern biblical discussion. An elaboration of the position taken here is not expedient in view of the aim of this book. For a presentation of the evidence that fornication is the sole scriptural reason for divorce and remarriage, see Thomas B. Warren, "There is One—and Only One—Ground for Divorce and Remarriage" in *Your Marriage Can Be Great,* Thomas B. Warren, ed. (Jonesboro, AR: National Christian Press, 1978), pp. 356-360. See also the article "Some More Crucial Questions Which Show The Distinction Between Truth and Error on Divorce and Remarriage" by the same author on pp. 387-402.

[17]Olan Hicks, *Divorce and Remarriage: The Issues Made Clear* (Searcy, AR: Gospel Enterprises, 1990), pp. 32-33.

[18]*Ibid.*

[19]*Ibid.*

. . . God's remedy for sin is to be sought and followed. If He did indeed pronounce remarriage a sin, it would then be wrong for the bereft partner to seek another mother or father for the children, and God would no doubt provide adequately for that missing link in the home. On the other hand, if the Bible does not see remarriage in such prudish terms, but as sometimes necessary under certain conditions, that avenue of forming a new union and home is God's perfect will. God's provision is always adequate to the need.[20]

Like Hicks' view of the needs of adults, Ellison's position is that the needs of children outweigh biblical restrictions on remarriage.

The chief obstacle to arriving at biblical answers to such matters is the emotionally supercharged nature of this issue. Marriage involves the strongest feelings between human beings, and those emotions quite often become the criteria for decision-making. Though the feelings evoked by this controversy may seem insuperable, God demands that they be subjugated to His will (Deut. 13:6-11; Luke 14:26). Particularly relevant is the occurrence of three biblical cases in which the severing of an illegitimate marital union was commanded. The marriage of David and Michal pointedly illustrates the requirements of divine law in the face of human emotions. From sinister motives Saul had given his daughter Michal to be David's wife (I Sam. 18:20-27; 19:11). While David was later fleeing from the jealous king, Saul gave Michal to Paltiel the son of Laish (I Sam. 25:44). She evidently entered an illegitimate marriage with this man, since he is later called her "husband":

So David sent messengers to Ishbosheth, Saul's son, saying, "Give me my wife Michal, whom I betrothed to myself for a hundred foreskins of the Philistines." And Ishbosheth sent and took her from her husband, from

---

[20]Stanley A. Ellison, *Divorce and Remarriage in the Church* (Grand Rapids, MI: Lamplighter Books, Zondervan Publishing House, 1977), p. 72.

> Paltiel the son of Laish. Then her husband went along
> with her to Bahurim, weeping behind her. So Abner said
> to him, "Go, return!" And he returned (II Sam. 3:14-16).

The tears of Paltiel in this story were no doubt real. The
relationship they had shared brought emotional closeness, and
it was extremely painful for him to break this tie. But the
feelings occasioned by this separation did not alter a central
fact: Michal was another man's wife. Paltiel had no right to be
married to her, and Saul had arranged this marriage in violation of the original marital covenant with David.

A similar example is the unscriptural union between Herod
and Herodias. This sinful relationship became the occasion for
the imprisonment and death of John the Baptist after he rebuked Herod (Luke 3:19-20):

> For Herod himself had sent and laid hold of John, and
> bound him in prison for the sake of Herodias, his brother
> Philip's wife; for he had married her. For John had said
> to Herod, "It is not lawful for you to have your brother's
> wife" (Mark 6:17-18).

Of particular importance in this account is the sense of the
word *married*. As used here, this word cannot mean marriage
as an authorized union in the sight of God, since John labeled
it an "unlawful" relationship. Also, Herod "married" his
brother's *wife*. The word *married* in this context, then, is used
accommodatively to denote a mere legal arrangement having
civil but not divine approval. The same sense occurs in divorce
and remarriage texts when Jesus says that to "marry" after an
unscriptural divorce is to commit adultery.

But it is impossible for a God-authorized, scriptural marriage to be equivalent to adultery, the very opposite of this holy
bond. It is this distinction that makes the appeal to I Corinthians
7:2, 9 in an attempt to justify unscriptural marriages invalid.
Paul is speaking in these verses of legitimate marriages; it is
absurd to argue that Paul here authorized the entering of
marriages that in other passages are said to constitute adultery.

The question of innocent children caught in unscriptural unions finds an instructive example in Ezra's time. Upon learning that the children of Israel had intermarried with the neighboring heathen countries, Ezra issued a decree of separation: "Now therefore, make confession to the Lord God of your fathers, and do his will; separate yourselves from the peoples of the land, and from the pagan wives" (Ezra 10:11). After a listing of those who were guilty of marrying pagan women, the record ends with the observation that "some of them had wives by whom they had children" (Ezra 10:44). If the familial needs of children may justify unbiblical marriages, then why did not Ezra instead refer to this factor as an overriding consideration, permitting those involved to remain in the unions mentioned?

Adding to the strength of this example in connection with unscriptural marriages today is the nature of the prohibition that called for the dissolution of these marriages. The basis for the law forbidding the Israelites to marry those of other nations (Deut. 7:1-4) was religious, not racial: "For they will turn your sons away from following Me, to serve other gods. . . ." (v. 4).

The true intent of this prohibition is especially apparent in the case of Ruth, a Moabitess who converted to the religion of Israel (Ruth 2:2, 12) and entered the lineage of Christ (Ruth 4:22; Matt. 1:5). Moses himself married an Ethiopian (Num. 12:1), and these cases show that interracial marriages under the law of Moses were not intrinsically sinful but were a matter of legislation involving positive law.

Adultery is intrinsically evil regardless of the biblical dispensation in which it occurs. This difference gives rise to a significant question: If familial needs did not qualify the Mosaic prohibition of international marriages, a case of divine positive law, then how could this factor qualify New Testament teaching which describes unscriptural remarriage as adultery—a matter of moral law?

While the plight of children placed in unholy unions not of their choosing is truly heart-rending, this circumstance does not override divine law regarding marriage. If the fact that children are involved in an unscriptural marriage justifies continuance in that union, then how could polygamous relationships in which children are involved be consistently opposed? If the consideration of children justifies adultery, then why could it not also justify polygamy? The reality of such circumstances is seen in a letter from an African man:

> . . . I married many wives all with children; there is no possibility of divorcing them because of the issue I have with them. What shall I do to solve this problem? Presently I am with six wives and twenty-one children.[21]

That the New Testament requires monogamy is clear (I Cor. 7:2; Matt. 19:4-9; Rom. 7:1-3), but many who would deny that the polygamist has a right to keep a plurality of wives because children are involved argue that those entering an adulterous marriage may continue in that union for the same reason.[22] People tend to judge matters according to their particular culture and realm of experience. Without honest self-appraisal and consistent application of Bible teaching, this tendency easily leads to biased judgment.

A modern scenario within our culture exposes the fallacy being considered. Suppose the husband of a childless couple has an affair and impregnates the other woman who happens to be single. If the familial needs of children outweigh biblical laws on marriage, would not the man be *obligated* to divorce his wife and marry his mistress to provide a home for his child? The absurdity of this course of action can be established only by a proper consideration of the relationship between the areas of duty.

That marriage is a more fundamental relationship that takes precedence over the parent-child tie is seen in its description as

[21]Roy Deaver, "Marriage, Divorce, And Remarriage" in *Moral Issues Confronting the Kingdom*, ed. Thomas F. Eaves (Knoxville, TN: Karns Church of Christ, 1978), p. 121.

[22]Ellisen, *Divorce and Remarriage in the Church*, pp. 58, 82, 69-76, 115-117; Olan Hicks, *The Connally-Hicks Debate* (Jonesboro, AR: National Christian Press, 1979), pp. 46, 57-59.

a one-flesh union (Matt. 19:4-6; Gen. 2:20-24), a designation in Scripture given to no other human relationship. While the father-son analogy is commonly used in the Bible to represent God and His people, it is the great mystery reflected by marriage that Paul uses to show the relationship between Christ and the church (Eph. 5:22-33).

In short, the need of children to have a home cannot be used to redefine the very relationship from which they are ideally to be born. Of course, the fact that a child is conceived illegitimately does not absolve either parent of all parental duties. But if the mother and father are barred from entering marriage because of biblical restrictions, circumstances limit the obligations normally enjoined. In the case of a married man fathering a child outside of wedlock, he should fulfill those obligations that he may legitimately meet, especially in the area of material support.

The passing of time is often alleged to have an altering effect on the status of a life situation. How could a loving God require a union to be dissolved when the couple have been married for years, children have been born in this relationship, and the family on the whole is happy?

This reasoning applied to other parallel questions exposes the faulty assumption it employs. Child kidnapping, for instance, has robbed some couples of their offspring. Suppose that a child stolen in infancy from his real parents spends his first years in the home of another couple. In the substitute home he finds security and love. However, the real parents finally locate their child through the efforts of investigators. When the child's surrogate parents are confronted with the evidence, they insist that the child should remain with them because of the bond that has developed. But their defense ignores a fundamental unchanged fact: the child does not now and has never belonged to them. The same principle applies to marriage. The passing of time did not make Herodias Herod's wife any more than the civil ceremony that occurred at the outset of their unlawful union.

An unintentional but factual case of marriage to a disallowed party is seen in a real life example in this century.[23] Anton and Anna Nakonecznyj were married in a Ukrainian village in 1942. When Anton was taken away by Nazi soldiers two years later, Anna began a long wait for his return. Nine years later, convinced that he was dead, she remarried. Anna was unaware, however, that after the war ended Anton was afraid to return to the Soviet Union or write his relatives. He finally discovered Anna's situation when he moved to the United States. After her second husband, by whom she had given birth to three children, died, Anton and she were reunited in marriage.

But what was Anna's state before the death of the second husband? Was she married to two men, and if not, to which man was she scripturally joined? The answers to such questions cannot be ascertained on the basis of feelings, since equally compelling emotional reasons could be advanced for either alternative. The scriptural fact is that she was still married to Anton from the very beginning, since neither death nor a scriptural divorce had occurred. The time that had elapsed, the children who had been born, and the closeness that had developed between Anna and the second man did not remove this underlying fact.

These examples represent unfamiliar and rare situations. It is precisely because most people have not experienced them that they are included in this discussion. Because of emotional separation from such experiences, most readers will be more objective in their assessment of these situations in terms of the application of the biblical principles involved. More importantly, they illustrate in modern terms the absolute status of God's law concerning divorce and remarriage.

[23]*LIFE* (New York, NY: Time Incorporated Magazine Company, 1992), March, 1992, p. 23.

The Abortion Controversy

For those accepting the Bible as the infallible guide to moral issues, the basic facts in the abortion controversy are clear. The Scriptures teach that life begins at conception. After Isaac prayed to the Lord, "Rebekah his wife conceived" (Gen. 25:21). The next words in the text are: "But the children struggled together within her" (v. 22). Elisabeth "conceived a son in her old age" (Luke 1:36)—a son or human being, not a mere substance that later became human (cf. Job 3:3; Ps. 51:5). From a purely logical standpoint, if life does not begin at conception, then why does the growth process begin at this point? The fetuses in Rebekah's womb were called "children"; the following verse records God's declaration to her: "Two nations are in your womb. . . ." (v. 23).

No distinction is made in the Scriptures between an unborn baby and a newborn infant as far as their status as human beings is concerned. John the Baptist is called a "babe" while inside his mother's womb (Luke 1:41, 44); Jesus is referred to by the same word (*brephos*) shortly after his birth (Luke 2:12). Other passages confirm that the growing fetus is a human being (Ps. 139:13-16; Job 31:15; Jer. 1:5). Since the unjust taking of human life is sinful, the malicious act of abortion amounts to murder.

Though these fundamental truths become evident after a minimal amount of investigating the Scriptures, the question arises whether qualifying considerations may justify abortion in some situations. Of the allegedly justifying circumstances offered in defense of abortion, those involving abortions for career reasons or because of financial burden have the least resemblance to any type of biblical support. The motivation behind such operations is sheer selfishness.

The question takes on an added emotional factor in pregnancies resulting from rape or incest. Though giving birth in these cases is a traumatic experience, psychological distress is a biblically unwarranted reason for having an abortion. The unborn child is a human being; the circumstances in which he was conceived do not make him any less so. While the mother did not choose to have this child, neither did the child choose to be brought into the world, and to take his life in this case is murder.

A further complication arises in the case of government-forced abortions such as those performed in compliance with China's one-child-per-family law. If civil law calls for abortion for population control, is it right to resist this law, especially since the Scriptures warn Christians not to rebel against rulers (Rom. 13:1-2)? At this point the actions of the apostles (Acts 5:29) and others (Dan. 3, 6) become pertinent. China's policy regarding the limiting of family members is a departure from the authorized realm of civil government and an intrusion into the function of the home as a God-ordained institution. Civil rulers have no right to demand citizens to abort babies.

Perhaps the most complex angle to this issue is whether abortion is permissible when the mother's life is endangered, as in the case of a tubal pregnancy or cancer of the uterus. Such cases are rare, but they do occur, and statistics showing their infrequency are neither instructive nor comforting to those facing these difficult situations. This painful reality is even more difficult in these cases because the issue of life and death involves two persons instead of one. If diagnosis indicates that the mother's life is actually at stake, two courses of action are possible. One is that no medical intervention is pursued and nature is allowed to take its course, resulting in the death of the mother and perhaps the child as well. The other is that action is taken so one life will be saved. Which alternative is biblical? If the second is the right course, whose life should be saved—the mother's or the child's?

Since no direct statements occur in Scripture on this question, the answer may be obtained only through a proper synthesis of relevant biblical principles. One such principle is the moral obligation to save human life. Jesus asked rhetorically, "Is it lawful on the Sabbath to do good or to do evil, to save life

or to kill" (Mark 3:4)? Noah is praised for his faith shown in
saving the lives of his family (Heb. 11:7); the Good Samaritan
exemplified the second greatest commandment by showing
mercy to the half-dead traveller (Luke 10:30-37). When opportunity is present, one should use the legitimate means available to fulfill this duty.

Another relevant factor is whether the Bible indicates a
relative scale of value in regard to the life of the mother and the
life of the child. If the mother's life can be shown by the
Scriptures to be more important than the life of the unborn
child, a significant criterion has been established.

A central passage concerning the relative value of the
mother's life is Moses' teaching in the following text:

> If men fight, and hurt a woman with child, so that she
> gives birth prematurely, yet no lasting harm follows, he
> shall surely be punished accordingly as the woman's
> husband imposes on him; and he shall pay as the judges
> determine. But if any lasting harm follows, then you
> shall give life for life, eye for eye, tooth for tooth, hand for
> hand, foot for foot, burn for burn, wound for wound,
> stripe for stripe (Ex. 21:22-25).

Two critical points in the interpretation of this passage are: (1)
the meaning of the clause "she gives birth prematurely"; (2)
the nature of the "harm" that follows. In regard to the first
point, more literal translations have "so that her fruit depart"
(KJV, ASV); the Septuagint has the strange rendering "and
her child be born imperfectly formed." The New English Bible
uses the word *miscarriage* while the New International Version relegates this term to a marginal note on the phrase. The
Hebrew reads "and her child (*yeled*) comes out (*yatsa*)." While
yatsa sometimes refers to giving birth (II Sam. 7:12; Gen.
35:11), it occurs over a thousand times in the Old Testament
and is used in a wide range of senses, each of which is determined by the context. Whether it refers in Exodus 21:22 to a
premature live birth or a miscarriage must be decided upon
this basis.

Ironically, the contextual evidence in this passage hinges on the word *harm* (the word *lasting* is supplied by the New King James Version translators). The Hebrew word is *ason*, a word used elsewhere only in reference to the "calamity" Jacob feared would fall upon Benjamin (Gen. 42:4, 38; 44:29). In Exodus 21, its contrast with *hurt* (v. 21) and the punishment prescribed in verse 23 indicate that it refers to death. But to whose death does the word *harm* refer?

Five conceivable answers might be given to this question. One is that the woman's death is signified by this word. In this scenario, if she did not die the man responsible would be fined; if she died his life would go for hers. Unless the clause "her child comes out" refers to a miscarriage, the man would not even be fined for the death of the baby. Since the unborn child was known to be a human being (cf. Gen. 25:21-23), such a complete failure to penalize the man does not appear likely.

The second position with regard to the word *harm* is that it refers solely to the death of the child. But this view entails a serious difficulty. If the harm that follows is the death of the child, then no punishment is given in the passage in case the woman dies.

The third possibility is that *harm* refers to the death of either the mother or the child. But this view is too narrow, since it does not cover the case of both the mother and the child dying in the accident.

The fourth suggestion is that this last situation—the death of both the mother and the child—is what is envisioned in the word *harm*. This position is too broad, since in this interpretation the punishment of verse 23 would apply only if both parties died.

The fifth alternative is to view this *harm* generally as referring to any death that might follow: either the death of the mother or the child or the death of both of them. But if this interpretation is correct, why would the phrase "so that she gives birth prematurely" be included in the legislation? Unless it refers to miscarriage, this part of the text is unnecessary in stating the circumstances of wrongdoing. It appears then that the harm in these verses is the death of the mother while the premature delivery refers to miscarriage. This interpretation fits most naturally with the events described in the text, since an injury to a pregnant woman serious enough to cause her to lose the child would probably result in the child's death,[24] especially in the absence of modern life-saving equipment.

A significant implication follows from this legislation. If the child dies, the penalty is a fine; if the mother dies, the punishment is the loss of the offender's life. This does not mean that the fetus is considered less than human in this passage. The verses previously cited showing that the unborn fetus is a human being rule out this suggestion. In addition, the mere fact that the offender was not capitally punished in verse 22 fails to establish that the fetus was subhuman in value because the death portrayed was unintentional.

But if the mother's death was also accidental, why did her death occasion a more severe penalty? The key seems to be in the reasoning that a greater degree of punishment implies a greater degree of guilt. But why was causing the mother's death more serious than causing the death of her child? Since the cause of either death was the same injury, the only factor that seems to warrant such a distinction is the relative worth of the mother's life in comparison to the life of the child. In terms of family roles, the death of the mother would be a

[24]This single contextual factor is weightier than the linguistic argument that "the Hebrew word for miscarriage, *shakal,* is not used here...Nothing in the text requires us to understand that the fetus is born dead" (James K. Hoffmeier, "Abortion and the Old Testament Law," *Abortion: A Christian Understanding and Response* [Grand Rapids, MI: Baker Book House, 1987], p. 59; cf. John Jefferson Davis, *Abortion and the Christian: What Every Believer Should Know* [Grand Rapids, MI: Baker Book House, 1984], p. 51 and John I Durham, *Word Biblical Commentary: Exodus* [Waco, TX: Word Books, Publisher, 1987] p. 324). This reasoning, though common, is circular, resting upon the assumption that since one word is "usually" employed to express a given idea, then this word would have been used if the writer had intended to convey the idea (as if *shakal* was the sole word at the author's disposal to communicate the concept of miscarriage).

greater loss than the death of the unborn infant. If the fetus dies, the family will grieve; but if the mother dies, the husband and other children who may have been born into the family suffer the loss of inestimable needs provided by her.

Sometimes the agonizing decision must be made as to which of two human beings should live when death is inevitable for one of them. During the sinking of the Titanic, more than eighty percent of those who drowned were men who surrendered their lifeboat seats to women and children.[25] The frightening reality of such a situation enables us to realize that the endangerment of a mother's life during pregnancy is not the only circumstance in which this difficult decision exists. If it is right to sacrifice life to save life in a shipwreck, then the same forfeiture could be made in regard to the expectant mother whose life will be lost if the pregnancy continues.

Obligations to Family Members

That we are to honor God above all others is consistently affirmed in the Scriptures. The God of Israel was a jealous God (Exod. 34:14), requiring that His people stone even the closest relatives or friends who attempted to turn them from the true God (Deut. 13:6-11). This priority of allegiance and affection is expressed in Jesus' ultimatum that His followers must "hate" (in a comparative sense) family members in order to be His disciples (Luke 14:26). Though a natural bond exists between family members, an unswerving commitment to God takes precedence over these ties, with the result often being that "a man's foes will be those of his own household" (Matt. 10:36).

It is also true that everyday duties regarding familial relations must sometimes give place to more urgent demands involving specific Christian responsibilities. The opportunity to hear the teaching of Christ took precedence over the domestic duties about which Martha was worried (Luke 10:38-42). During the earthly life of Christ, the apostles had "left all" to

[25]*TIME* (New York, NY: Time Incorporated Magazine Company, 1992), April 27, 1992, p. 22.

follow Him (Mark 10:28). In response, Jesus promised that those who had left "house or brothers or sisters or father or mother or wife or children or lands" would be blessed a hundredfold in this life in addition to receiving eternal life (Mark 10:29-30).

Cultic mishandling of these passages has resulted in a distorted view of the role of the home and the responsibilities of its members. In their characteristic attempt to isolate members from associations outside the group, cult leaders often twist these verses to dissuade followers from maintaining family ties, since these connections are seen as a threat to the goals of the cult. One former member of such a group testifies that:

> At one time during my five-year membership in the Children of God/Family of Love, I showed too much affection for my parents. As a result, I was subjected to days of intensive, intimidating, and humiliating "counseling" sessions staged by the leaders to correct my "spiritual problem." The sessions were continued until I capitulated and, at least outwardly, denounced my parents.[26]

This type of separation is expected while children are living with their parents. A young lady who became a member of a movement known as "Crossroads" among churches of Christ later complained that

> to them anything that was not church work—or rather, what *they* perceived as church work—was sinful. Therefore, washing dishes, cleaning my room, helping mom with chores, or simply being at home with my family were all "unscriptural" or so I was constantly told. Henry would say, "That's not the best emphasis a true Christian should have. Jesus said we are to hate our mother and father if they keep us from following him. That means to disobey them if you have to."[27]

[26]Una McManus and John Cooper, *Dealing With Destructive Cults* (Grand Rapids, MI: Zondervan Publishing House, 1984), p. 49.

[27]Bronwen McClish Gibson, *Crossroads From the Inside* (Denton, TX: Valid Publications, Incorporated, 1988) p. 16.

Even casual reflection on the overall teaching of Scripture exposes the dishonesty behind this perversion of Jesus' words. How could Jesus tell His disciples to literally hate family members when Paul commands love between them (Eph. 5:25-33; Titus 2:3-5)? Jesus upheld the Old Testament principle of honoring one's parents (Matt. 15:3-6). To assign the usual sense of the word *hate* to Luke 14:26 is to place Jesus in contradiction with Himself. The word is used by Christ in this verse in a comparative sense and means "to love less" (cf. Gen. 29:30-31).

A distortion created by cultic misinterpretation of Scripture is the illegitimate separation made between "duties to God" and "duties to family members." The connotation given to "service to God" is limited to activities of the group such as evangelistic programs and group devotionals. One advocate of the Crossroads philosophy wrote that "some parents, even some Christian parents, just do not understand biblical concepts like total commitment, surrender, Lordship, discipleship, and living sacrifice."[28] The fallacy inherent in this mentality is that these concepts may be fulfilled only in such activities as soul-winning, Bible study, and worship services. The implication is that these activities are aspects of Christian service, while ordinary responsibilities such as housekeeping, rest, and manual labor are less spiritual endeavors. But these everyday activities are part of Christian living (Titus 2:5; Mark 6:31; II Thess. 3:10-12). The false dichotomy constructed by cultists ignores a fundamental truth stated by Paul: "Therefore, whether you eat or drink, or whatever you do, do all to the glory of God" (I Cor. 10:31).

Aside from these more obvious misrepresentations of biblical teaching, another difficulty involving familial responsibilities emerges when these duties are considered in light of Paul's command to "withdraw from every brother who walks disorderly" (II Thess. 3:6, 14-15; I Cor. 5:1-13). If the person to be

[28]Robert Nelson, *Understanding the Crossroads Controversy* (Fort Worth, TX: Star Bible Publications, Incorporated, 1981), p. 142.

disfellowshipped is the husband or wife of a faithful member of the congregation, what is the Christian's responsibility? Does Paul's admonition apply to a Christian woman whose husband has been disciplined? If so, then the injunction "do not keep company with him" (II Thess. 3:14) also applies, since this instruction is an element of the withdrawal procedure. She also could not eat a common meal with him, since this is also forbidden by Paul (I Cor. 5:11). In short, if these passages apply to the Christian wife of a disciplined husband, her duty would be to separate from him.

Though a wife in this predicament is to continue to admonish the wayward husband, she cannot "withdraw" from him without violating Jesus' warning: "What God has joined together, let not man separate" (Matt. 19:6; cf. I Cor. 7:10-11). What should be remembered is that two separate realms are involved in this case—the church and the home. While the divine intention is that these institutions should complement each other, neither is to cause the dissolution of the other. Bible teaching on corrective discipline does not undermine so fundamental a relationship as marriage. This fact is no less true when the disciplined family member is a parent or a teenage son or daughter at home. These persons cannot avoid having "company" with each other; the Bible obligates each person in the home to maintain a warm, peaceful environment (Eph. 5:22-6:4; Col. 3:18-21). The primacy of the relationships in the home qualifies the duty to discipline disorderly church members.

8

Are There Qualifications
of the Principle
# of Qualification?

Qualification: A Means For Justifying Any Belief?

A frequent charge of skeptics is that theists use qualification as a convenient means to evade the force of contrary evidence. In the brief but influential article, *Theology and Falsification*,[1] Antony Flew argued that such statements as "God answers prayer" and "God loves mankind" have been qualified to the point that they no longer have verifiable meaning. In a debate on the existence of God with Thomas B. Warren, Flew claimed that

> . . . it is possible to start with some assertions about the existence of something, but then to put in various qualifications which make your assertion less and less one that could be tested at all . . . For instance, people affirm confidently that prayer is always answered. But then they say, "Yes, but sometimes the answer is no." Well, when one has done that, and unless one has got some method of determining that the answer is no, provides a distinction between a no answer—you know, say, "No, you shan't have that" and no answer at all, one has

[1]Antony Flew, "Theology and Falsification," *The Existence of God*, John Hick, ed. (New York, NY: Macmillan Publishing Company, 1964), pp. 225-228.

qualified one's original assertion in such a way that it is
no longer possible to test whether it is true or not.[2]

Flew contends that the result of such exception-making is that
the believer's original statement is "so eroded by qualification"
that it is "no longer an assertion at all."[3] It has become void of
any meaning, having suffered "death by a thousand qualifications."[4]

A similar charge is made concerning the claim that God
loves mankind. When this claim is countered by someone pointing to "a child dying of inoperable cancer of the throat . . . Some
qualification is made—God's love is 'not a merely human love'
or it is 'an inscrutable love' . . ."[5] The thrust of the falsification
argument is that no matter how compelling the atheist's
counter-evidence is, the theist averts the weight of this evidence by endlessly redefining propositions, leaving the theistic
position beyond the reach of testability.

The central issue at stake is the meaning of testability or
verification. Who decides whether or not a proposition is testable and by what criteria this decision is made? In Flew's case,
the underlying assumption is one which has its roots in a
theory known as logical positivism. This system holds that
statements fall into one of three categories: (1) analytic or
tautologous statements such as "all triangles are three-sided
figures" or "all bachelors are unmarried men"; (2) synthetic
statements, which may be verified by the senses; (3) meaningless statements. Since assertions about God fall into neither of
the first two classes, they are considered nonsensical by logical
positivists. Like all anti-biblical views, this theory is its own
death knell. By its own categorization, logical positivism is a
meaningless theory, since it does not fall into either of the first
two categories. Flew's falsification argument is merely an off-
shoot of this view. His case rests upon his definition of verifica-

[2]Thomas B. Warren and Antony G. N. Flew, *The Warren-Flew Debate on
the Existence of God* (Jonesboro, AR: National Christian Press, 1977), p. 23.
[3]Flew, *Theology and Falsification*, p. 227.
[4]*Ibid.*, p. 226.
[5]*Ibid.*, p. 227.

tion, but he makes no attempt to prove this concept. When Warren applied the falsification argument to Flew's own atheistic position, Flew admitted that his view might in theory be falsified.[6] The qualifications of the theistic claim that God exists criticized by Flew are not beyond testing. They are simply not testable by Flew's standards of verification.

Though Flew's attack upon theistic qualifications is unwarranted because of the assumptions it carries, there is an actual sense in which the principle of qualification is misused in religious controversy. Overly zealous adherents of a belief system often dismiss logical contradictions in their doctrine at all costs, even at the expense of plain reason. They "solve" the inconsistency by arbitrarily redefining one or both of the conflicting statements. The words in question become clay in their hands. They are intelligent enough to realize that theology must be consistent within itself but not honest enough to admit that such is not characteristic of their system. Statements as delivered in their original contexts are constantly amended to give the appearance of internal consistency. The alleged qualification also may take the form of circular reasoning, as when the argument is made that those who seem to have fallen from grace were never actually saved (since saved people do not fall—the very point in question)!

Communication would be impossible if language were abused in this manner in other areas of life. Unless words have a fixed reference of meaning, they fail to convey a thought which is capable of being interpreted with any certainty. But the fact that such reasoning is shunned by the zealous apologists noted above when it occurs in other contexts shows that a different type of problem exists. For instance, such people are shocked by the ingenuity of a liar who, when confronted about the inconsistency of his statements, always seems to find a way out of a dilemma by reinterpreting his original statements. Do his tactics differ from religious people who are unwilling to face a

[6]Anthony Flew and Thomas B. Warren, *The Warren-Flew Debate*, pp. 92-98, 103.

contradiction in their theology? Like the lawyer who asked, "And who is my neighbor" (Luke 10:29)? because he desired to justify himself, some look for any semblance of escape from a logical difficulty in a cherished belief. Instead of "rightly dividing the word of truth" (II Tim. 2:15), they "twist" the Scriptures to their own hurt (II Pet. 3:16).

Does the Principle Have Practical Value in Choosing the Better of Two Good Actions?

Much of the discussion to this point has focused on qualification as it applies to negative commands. But does the principle also assist one in deciding between two obligations that appear to be equally important? Such decisions frequently present themselves to Christians on a personal level: Should I stay at home with my family tonight or hold a group Bible study with an interested couple I met at work today? How could my time be better spent this afternoon—in Bible study and prayer or in visiting the sick? To what noble cause will I leave part of my inheritance: a foreign mission, a desperate orphanage, a struggling Christian school, or an impoverished church? Similar choices exist on a professional level in selecting a specialized area of Christian service and in performing the numerous duties it requires: What field of work should I enter: preaching, counseling, missions, benevolence, Christian education, or some other area? What about the idea of specializing? Are the sacrifices of other legitimate interests to concentrate on a particular concern justified?

Of the biblical factors affecting such decisions, the question of ability and talent plays a major role. The mere limitations of physical circumstances serve to reduce the number of options from which to choose. A bedridden saint does not enjoy the privilege of visiting others; a poor Christian has less to decide about giving than a wealthy brother or sister. Similarly, though lack of special talent in a particular area of Christian service does not remove responsibility altogether, it does point to a different direction as far as full-time Christian service is concerned. The Bible indicates that some have more talent in given areas than others. Aside from the supernatural gift of prophecy, Paul's list of talents in Romans 12 are natural endowments:

> Having then gifts differing according to the grace that is given to us, let us use them: if prophecy, let us prophesy in proportion to our faith; or ministry, let us use it in our ministering; he who teaches, in teaching; he who exhorts, in exhortation; he who gives, with liberality; he who leads, with diligence; he who shows mercy, with cheerfulness (vv. 6-8).

Closely connected with this aspect of the problem is the role that God's providence plays in such decisions. Although this element of human life is no grounds for shirking responsibility in decision-making, it is a contributing factor in the final outcome of the course of human events. In a manner consistent with the free will of man, God may providentially limit the number of physical possibilities available to an individual. Also, in addition to naturally endowing men with special capabilities, God may refine character and develop talent by life experience.

Since God has a hand in earth life, praying to Him for wisdom (James 1:5) and for providential assistance (James 5:16-18) is an indispensable part of Christian ethics. Choosing a career or a marriage partner is too monumental a decision to make without prayerful reliance on the providence of God. Even in less consequential choices, entering decisions with the recognition of God's involvement in the world provides the comfort of knowing that "all things work together for good to those who love God" (Rom. 8:28).

The interpretational basis of such decisions involves important practical guidelines arising out of the principle of qualification. One is the element of priority. Which course of action is the more fundamentally important? Which option will bring the greatest amount of good? That some duties take precedence over others has already been shown, especially in such passages as Matthew 23:23 and Mark 12:29-31. This factor should be scripturally assessed in decisions involving more than one good alternative.

Another concern that is particularly difficult for paid church workers to maintain is balance. Any legitimate Christian activity can become excessive and realizing when this line has been crossed is seldom easy. Every conscientious preacher wrestles with this problem. A steady input of a variety of scriptural information coupled with the practice of biblical teaching in interaction with others helps to maintain this balance. Also, the distinction between needs and preferences must be acknowledged and upheld. What we would like to do often must give way to what we need to do, even when the preferred action is legitimate in itself. Though he desired to depart and be with Christ, Paul recognized that to remain on earth was "more needful" for the brethren (Phil. 1:23-24). This distinction is also at work in the contents of the book of Jude. While purposing to write a general epistle about "the common salvation," Jude realized the presence of a more urgent problem: the threat of false teachers (Jude 4). As a result, he penned a more specific letter in which he explained to his readers: "I found it necessary to write to you exhorting you to contend earnestly for the faith which was once for all delivered to the saints" (Jude 3).

Do Ethical Dilemmas Actually Occur on the Practical Level?

An important distinction should be made between theoretical and virtual dilemmas in Christian ethics. This book has dealt with the question of ethical dilemmas on the level of theory, maintaining that God's commandments do not come into conflict so as to leave one without a "way of escape" (I Cor. 10:13). But while objective ethical dilemmas are precluded by this fact, subjective dilemmas in real life situations do occur. One may in facing a complex circumstance be unaware as to which of the alternatives is proper. For all practical purposes, the situation is to him a dilemma. Also, one may be unable to foresee the consequences of the possible courses of action in a case in which this factor appears to be the only criterion. In the world of practice, a lack of knowledge creates virtual dilemmas. Since no one possesses a quick answer to every perplexing situation of life, such dilemmas are practically inevitable.

While the thought of virtual dilemmas is frightening, this element of life serves important spiritual purposes. Constituting a critical test of the human spirit, practical dilemmas are conducive to spiritual growth. Difficult circumstances motivate the Christian to find the answer in the Scriptures. These challenges constantly drive the Christian back to the Word for knowledge and encouragement. Once found, the answer can then be shared with others. Experience and Bible study work cooperatively in maintaining this cycle. As a result, leadership qualities are forged in the perseverant child of God. For instance, the wisdom of God in requiring that elders first learn to manage their families (I Tim. 3:4-5) is appreciated most by men who occupy this office. How often are the problems encountered in shepherding a flock of God's people in principle the same as those faced in managing a family? How valuable is the wisdom and patience that are acquired through wrestling with a decision that offered no easy solution? The level of spiritual strength we desire is gained in the refining heat of trials. Virtual dilemmas test the character of man, bringing out either the best or the worst in him.

Dilemmas as a virtual reality of life also serve as a reminder of our dependence upon God. In situations that offer no easy solution, the conscientious child of God quickly realizes his own inadequacy. He is driven to his knees, humbled before the God of heaven to whom he cries out for mercy and assistance. By encountering the dilemma, he is made painfully aware of the limitations of human wisdom. A feeling of utter helplessness impels him to come to the throne of grace to "obtain mercy and find grace to help in time of need" (Heb. 4:16). God looks at sins committed through ignorance and weakness differently than He does at deliberate transgressions (I John 1:7-10; Heb.

10:26). As a merciful Father, He is patient with those who fear Him (Ps. 103:8-18).

The admission that virtual dilemmas do occur does not remove the need for this book. I have not argued in the preceding pages that Christians will always know the biblical answer to difficult moral decisions. I have instead maintained that God cannot be blamed for any such dilemmas and that the ethical system of the Bible is perfect. There is a vast difference between saying that an apparent conflict between God's commands is irresolvable and saying that a given person cannot resolve the difficulty. The first statement impugns the Author of Scripture; the second reflects the weakness of man. If one has a faulty view of this subject on the theoretical level, his application of biblical principles to life situations will be tainted. Rather than denying the need for this study, the fact that practical dilemmas occur places an examination of this kind in a balanced perspective. While our knowledge and practice of the biblical system of ethics is imperfect, the system itself is perfect. With assurance we can say, "Your word is a lamp to my feet and a light to my path" (Ps. 119:105).

Bibliography

Aquinas, Thomas. *Summa Theologica.* Westminster, MD: Christian Classics, 1981 reprint.

Archer, Gleason L. *Encyclopedia of Bible Difficulties.* Grand Rapids, MI: Zondervan Publishing House, Regency Reference Library, 1982.

Augustine. "On Lying." *A Select Library of the Nicene and Post-Nicene Fathers of the Christian Church,* Philip Schaff, ed. Grand Rapids, MI: William B. Eerdmans Publishing Company, 1980 reprint. Vol. III.

Berkhof, Louis. *Principles of Biblical Interpretation.* Grand Rapids, MI: Baker Book House, 1950.

Boyd, Gregory A. "The Divine Wisdom of Obscurity: Pascal on the Positive Value of Scriptural Difficulties." *The Journal of the Evangelical Theological Society.* Jackson, MS: The Evangelical Theological Society, June, 1985.

Fletcher, Joseph. *Situation Ethics: The New Morality.* Philadelphia, PA: Westminister Press, 1966.

Geisler, Norman L. *Christian Ethics: Options and Issues.* Grand Rapids, MI: Baker Book House, 1989.

Haley, John W. *Alleged Discrepancies of the Bible.* Nashville, TN: Gospel Advocate Company, 1974.

Hodge, Charles. *Systematic Theology.* Grand Rapids, MI: William B. Eerdmans Publishing Company, 1982 reprint. Vol. III.

Horne, Thomas Hartwell. *An Introduction to the Critical Study and Knowledge of the Holy Scriptures.* Grand Rapids, MI: Baker Book House, 1970 reprint. Vol. I, pt. 1.

Kierkegaard, Soren. *Fear and Trembling and the Sickness Unto Death*. Garden City, NY: Doubleday and Company, 1954.

_____. *Philosophical Fragments*. Princeton, NJ: Princeton University Press, 1962.

Murray, John. *Principles of Conduct: Aspects of Biblical Ethics*. Grand Rapids, MI: William B. Eerdmans Publishing Company, 1957.

Pink, Arthur W. *Interpretation of the Scriptures*. Grand Rapids, MI: Baker Book House, 1972.

Ramm, Bernard. *Protestant Biblical Interpretation: A Textbook of Hermeneutics*. Grand Rapids, MI: Baker Book House, 1970.

Thielicke, Helmut. *Theological Ethics: Foundations*. Grand Rapids, MI: William B. Eerdmans Publishing Company, 1966.